Profaned

Pulpit

The Jack Schaap Story©

by
Jerry D. Kaifetz, Ph.D.

SBN-13: 978-1479180295
ISBN-10: 1479180297

Written and published in the United States of America

Cover by Peg Lukas

TABLE OF CONTENTS

Lot, was "vexed with the filthy conversation of the wicked."

2 Peter 2:7

INTRODUCTION

This is a book I did not want to write. When my wife suggested in mid-August of 2012 that I write a book about Jack Schaap, I did not have a good reaction. I no more wanted to immerse myself into the degradation and stench of the swamp that Jack Schaap's life had become than I would want to jump into a sewer. I had tried to sound a warning to the man, but my letter (published in the Appendix) was ignored.

Then I began to talk to people like my good friend of twenty-five years, Voyle Glover, who said to me, "Well, you are certainly well positioned to write a book about Schaap, and I think it would help a lot of people." Those words had an impact on me, and when the Holy Spirit chimed in with a "he's right," (as He often did in conversations with Voyle) my entire perspective on the book changed. I knew I had just been painted into a corner, and if my spiritual insight had a physical dimension, I would have been able to see Jesus standing by the door of the room with a dripping paintbrush in His hand and a grin on His face. I knew better than to resist.

So I did what I knew to do: I wrote an outline. This would be my twelfth book. In about three minutes or less, I had my chapter outline scribbled on a yellow page-size piece of paper. I sat down at my keyboard and in about two hours, the first chapter was done. I printed it out and handed it to my wife and said, "Here, read this." She couldn't believe what I was doing.

Later that day I knocked out chapter two. The next morning the Lord woke me up at 4:00 a.m. and said to me: "WRITE!" (No, it was not an audible voice . . .)

The next day was Sunday and I went to church with three chapters in the can. The next morning, the same thing happened. God thought that by 3:30 a.m. I had enough sleep, and by 7:00 a.m. another chapter was being slung out of my printer. This pace continued, and in five days, the book was largely done. More than once along the way, I felt the close presence Holy Spirit as I wrote. I have to tell you, there are few feelings in life that can match that one, especially when you pull the pages out of the printer and your first thought is, "Did I write that?" Of course, in no way do I mean to imply divine inspiration here! I only want to say that I had some important help along the way.

The reason this book flowed out the way it did was because I had lived this crisis for more than twenty-five years. I had known Jack Hyles well, and I once had a close relationship with Jack Schaap, both personal and professional. I had also for years counseled the abused victims of First Baptist Church of Hammond and I had seen the stark realities the damages inflicted on women, children and families. I had heard myself the vulgarities and coarseness that had been expressed from the pulpit by Jack Schaap. I was horrified by it, but not surprised. I knew that his power and authority were unchecked and that the men on the platform were little more than bobble-head dolls. They had been programmed by the master programmer, Jack Hyles, to just nod in assent to anything delivered by the oracle in the pulpit, no matter how insane, no matter how ungodly, or how offensive to a holy God.

This book is the fruit of that outrage. What is most important, it is my attempt to reach out to the victims and to orient them in the direction of Jesus Christ as He stands at their door bathed in a cleansing and holy light, ready to make anyone who will reach out to Him whole with a cleansing, healing and regenerating hug that penetrates to the marrow. That embrace can be a daily ritual for anyone who will open their arms to Jesus Christ.

1

The Early Days

It was a hot summer day in Azle, Texas. The date was July 20, 1985. This date became one of the most important dates in my life. I had just flown from Chicago to Dallas for a very special occasion. There was excitement in the air, and much of that energy was coming from me. This was the first time our family was getting together in many years. It was the first time I had seen my best friend Bruce from Colorado in a long time. My mother and father were going to be there after many years of separation. My brother, Danny was going to be there. Even my cousin Jean Jack Chevalier from Paris had come with his wife. I was thirty-seven years old, never been wed, and I was getting married!

This occasion was shaping up to be the perfect and joyous day. I had traveled all over the world my entire life, though never as a tourist. I was born in Paris France, the first child of an American soldier with two Bronze Stars, and a beautiful French war bride, Janine Bonnet. My mother was the very first war bride to come to America. Her photo in a full length fur coat and long dark hair flowing went international as she walked down the stairs from the first passenger westbound transatlantic flight in history on Feb. 7, 1946. The plane was called "Star of Paris." As the first war bride, my mother was the first one to disembark. Mayor LaGuardia waited to greet her, the event making the front page of the New York

Times and papers around the world the next day. She was the showcase poster girl of French war brides.

My mother and father were both there that day in that little Texas church. There was also one other very special person there. He had gotten to the church before I did, even after his thousand mile flight from Chicago. When I walked into the church, he was sitting very casually on the edge of the platform to the right of the pulpit. He was the young preacher who was there to perform the ceremony. This was the first wedding he would perform. He was my best friend. It was a glorious day, and he did a masterful job. His name was Jack Schaap.

Jack Schaap and I had met two years earlier when I came to Northwest Indiana from San Diego to attend Hyles-Anderson College. I was a brand new Christian, coming to the Christian faith somewhat late in life at the age of thirty-five. I had been raised in two cultures: French and American. I had traveled the world over for my entire life and been educated in public schools in both countries. I learned French before English, which I learned at age six. I had been a professional skier for several years, after fifteen years of amateur ski racing in the United States.

I wound up in Europe again in those years, skiing and competing in France, Italy and Switzerland. My summers were spent in places like the French West Indies, the French Riviera and the Red Sea. It never cost me a dime. Most of the time I was paid to be there. My life was set against a background of continental glamour and elegant luxury in those days. I could travel on the largest fleet of private charter jets in the world and go more or less any place in the world that I chose and invite anyone I chose to come along. All my meals were served in indescribably elegant restaurants and prepared by French chefs thrice daily. Once on my boss's birthday we spent $30,000 on a dinner in a beautiful restaurant on the shores of a Carribean island. Having grossed six million dollars in five months, this sum was a mere pittance for us.

In addition to the sports in my life, I was also developing a career as an entertainer and even received a job offer in that field in Europe one year. The world was my playground.

My testimony bears record of this former life. With all of the glamour, excitement and luxury, there came a time, however, when I realized that my life was empty and had no meaning or purpose beyond the superficial. There was nothing more for the world to offer me. My world of million dollar yachts, celebrities flocking to my playgrounds, and luxury and opulence on every side, eventually brought me to the understanding that there was something missing. I could not define it, but neither could I deny the void in my life.

When I came to a saving faith in Jesus Christ in a little Baptist Church in San Diego, on April 10th, 1983, I came to an immediate conclusion. I knew that if Christ was whom He claimed, if He did what the Bible says, He did it for the world. So if the consequences of falling short of the great redemption He brought this world are what they appear to be, then nothing makes any sense except to dedicate my life to His cause. I sought guidance and counsel from my pastor, Pastor Dorman Owens, and I packed up everything and came to Hyles-Anderson College in the Fall of 1983. That is where I met Jack Schaap.

Schaap and I became good friends. Few, if any of the 2,300 students then in the college were as close to him as I was. He visited in our home, and we were invited to his 30th birthday party at his home in St. John, Indiana. I was in the living room when his father-in-law, Jack Hyles handed him a large gift-wrapped package. It did not seem strange to anyone that his mother-in-law Beverly Hyles was not there. People had gotten used to rarely seeing Mrs. Hyles with her husband, other than when she sat behind him every Sunday in the center-front seat in the 100+ member choir at First Baptist Church of Hammond. She sat there every Sunday in her Sunday best, right across the aisle from Jenny Nischick, her husband's secretary. There we no higher positions of power and prestige for a woman than to sit in those seats before an adoring crowd of thousands that had come to listen to their pastor preach the thundering messages that had made him nationally famous. It would have been unthinkable, perhaps even tantamount to sacrilegious, for any one to think that Hyles was flanked by his wife on one side, and his mistress on the other. My wonderful and treasured friend Vic Nischick had not yet written his book, *The Wizard of God*, describing with the full support of his family, that infamousand ongoing liaison.

Everyone knew that whatever was in that large giftwrapped package that Jack Hyles had just handed to his son-in-law on the occasion of his 30th birthday would be the gift of the day. Though he pleaded austerity regularly, lived in a modest house, and was fond of letting people know he owned no car and "drove the church mail wagon," Jack Hyles had amassed a sizeable fortune from his publishing empire. Many have claimed it was in the range of $25 million at the time of his death on February 6, 2001.

Schaap opened the package and took out a large, brown leather gun belt filled with large caliber bullets. In the holster was the biggest handgun I had ever seen: a massive .44 magnum caliber chrome revolver Everyone's mouth fell open. Hyles said, "Put in on, Jack!" Schaap stood up and hung that long gun belt around his twenty-nine-inch waist. When Hyles saw all the extra belt left over, he burst into a raucous and powerful laugh. He was laughing so hard that he could barely get the words out: "You're going to have to wrap it around yourself twice, Jack!" Then he started laughing even harder.

All of us there held Schaap in such high esteem, though not on the level of Hyles, that we did not know how to react. He was being mocked and ridiculed in his own home, in front of his closest friends and his wife, on his own birthday. It was a truly awkward position in which to find oneself. You couldn't join in the mockery of the man who had so honored you with the inestimable privilege of having been invited to his home for such a very special event. Here, however, was the man that you and everyone you knew venerated and nearly worshiped going nearly hysterical with laughter at your host's expense. We were all extremely relieved when that moment passed. It later occurred to me that Hyles was one of the early pioneers of the art of "regifting:" giving to others gifts that he had himself received as gifts. Hyles was inundated with gifts from pastors all over America. Since he had no life outside of his church and his nationwide ministry, there was very little the man could ever use, so he recycled as gifts much of what was given to him.

So here on the edge of the platform of a little Baptist church in Azle, Texas sat Jack Schaap, the man who had traveled two thousand miles round trip to marry my wife Gwen and me in 1985. There is no way to convey the enormous honor and lofty privilege that this represented for us. He was not only married to Hyles' daughter Cindy, not only a Vice President of Hyles-Anderson College and the most dynamic and popular preacher there, but there was no doubt in anyone's mind that he was the heir apparent to the incredibly vast religious empire of Jack Hyles. Five thousand pastors would flock every year to Hyles' Pastor's School to hear him tell how he had built one of the world's largest churches long before the term "megachurch" became a part of the American lexicon. He claimed a membership of 20,000 back then, and every Sunday he filled a 5,000 seat auditorium to capacity. Hyles was also the author of numerous books on everything from marriage and child rearing to church building.

Jack Schaap would later become my business partner. I ran out of funds a couple of years into my education at Hyles-Anderson College, and after much thought and some research, he suggested to me that the truck washing business was a field that showed good potential. I remember him telling me that as he sat at a car rental counter in an airport that far more people flocked to Budget Car rental than the other companies. I took his advice and with $50 worth of hoses, buckets and brushes, I set up shop at a truck stop on highway 41 in St. John, Indiana in 1986. The name of my company was "Budget Mobile Truck Wash."

I became very successful very quickly. When Schaap saw how successful, he suggested that I should consider franchising my business. I was content to see the business do what I had established it to do: pay my way through college. Then he came to me one day and told me that there was a man in the church looking for a startup business who had some money to invest. Soon we had a written contract with this man. I put him in business with everything he needed to succeed. I trained him and gave him $30,000 worth of customer accounts, a fully equipped truck, and he agreed to pay us $25,000. Schaap and I split the profits evenly. (More on that in a later chapter.)

So this was how I got to know the man, Jack Schaap. This was a friendship that I valued highly. It became the assumption by most people in that college and church environment that I was headed for a prominent career at First Baptist Church of Hammond. I would later become the only college student ever to teach in Pastor's School. I was the only college student to write a book, for which Hyles wrote the Introduction. That book was *"World Class Truth,"* first published in 1989. I have to be honest at this point and say that there was absolutely nothing that I saw in Jack Schaap at that time in his life that gave me any cause for concern. He was unparalleled as a preacher. He had been mentored and meticulously honed by

Hyles himself, and he had learned well. He taught homiletics at the college. There could not have been a more qualified person to teach the art and technique of powerful, effective preaching than Jack Schaap. I had some of Hyles' lessons on the subject, including "how to make yourself cry at will in a sermon," but Schaap had dissected the art of preaching in amazing detail and was himself a formidable preacher even in his early years. When he walked onto the chapel platform at Hyles-Anderson College, the roar of thunderous applause from the students made it abundantly clear: Jack Schaap was our rock star.

Now I stood before him in a tuxedo awaiting the moment when my beautiful bride, Gwen would walk down the aisle of that little Texas church in a flowing white wedding gown, and my best friend would perform our wedding ceremony in front of our assembled families. I felt bathed in the shimmering light of God's blessings. I had given my life to the cause of Jesus Christ, and in all honesty, I had held nothing back. I was fully invested and wanted only to do more. After twenty-nine years, that sentiment has not changed. Today I can echo the sentiment of some of the old timers who used to say, "I'm drinking from my saucer, because my cup has overflowed."

As the light of a hot Texas July afternoon shone through the little church windows, God seemed to be confirming to me, ***"I am a rewarder of those who diligently seek Me."***

We moved back to Texas in 2011, and we now live off a road called Azle Highway. Nearly three decades later, I look back on that day and remember that message that God whispered in my ear. I remember standing with my best friend beside me awaiting the woman with whom I would spend the rest of my life. With those memories, only one thought comes to my mind: I have been blessed indeed!

"Sadly, he believed the praises and adulation that the fawning crowds laid weekly at his feet instead of the mantra of John the Baptist: 'He must increase, and I must decrease.'"

Chapter

2

I Don't Fall

After coming back from a winter of ski racing in Europe in my early thirties, I felt it was time to retire from Alpine skiing competition. When I put an ad in the San Diego paper to sell my racing skis, I attracted the attention of some local ski racers in Southern California because my skis were U.S. Ski Team issue. One thing led to another and I eventually agreed to be their "ringer" for one of their team races. When I put my skis in the starting gate and once again and heard the starting cadence of the race starter, I knew I was not at all ready to give up ski racing. It was still in my blood.

The following winter I was still racing with these new friends I had made. There was a provision in the race series that each racer could throw out his worst performance of the season. I remember having this conversation with the Race Director:

JK: "You know, this rule about being able to throw out your worst race actually places someone like me at a disadvantage over the other racers."
RD: "How is that?"
JK: "Well, these guys are all in their early twenties and pretty short on racing experience. I am ten years older than most of them, just back from racing in Europe, and my style is much more steady and conservative than these younger guys. I

don't take wild chances in every race. I doubt if I will have a race that is so bad that I will want to throw it out. Knowing they can throw out a bad race I think makes them take more chances and gives them an advantage over someone like me."
RD: "Yes, but you could fall. If you do, you'll be glad you get to throw that race out."

I remember so well looking right at him and saying: "I don't fall."

From my personal perspective, I was right. In Europe, I had some top ten finishes against racers with World Cup experience. I had been racing for fifteen years as an amateur in high school and college and had been internationally ranked. I also had three years of Nordic jumping experience on the collegiate level. I couldn't remember the last time I had fallen in a race.

For those of you who could not help but get ahead of me here, I don't have to tell you what happened in my race that day: big-time crash! It was as if it all happened in slow motion. Even after I started going down, I refused to accept the outcome. I fought and contorted like a madman trying to get my skis back under me and balance my upper body over their center. It was too late. In a few milliseconds, some introductions were made: "Hello, snow, this is Jerry's face." "Hello, Jerry's face, this is Ice and Snow. We are not big on shaking hands, but we do rearrange facial features and we also love to whack ski racers into semi-consciousness."

This was one of these this-is-not-supposed-to-happen-to-me events. I was stunned and humiliated. My teammates tried to cheer me up and told me, "Hey, this happens to everybody." My answer was, "Yeah, but it happens to other racers; not to me."

Falling on my face in such a humiliating way reminded me

many years later of one the great Bible doctrines so ignored in Fundamentalism: The Doctrine of the Total Depravity of Man. The outcome of understanding this doctrine can yield the kind of sentiment that was never better expressed than by John the Baptist in reference to his cousin, Jesus of Nazareth. John said, *"He must increase, and I must decrease."* I used to say about Jack Hyles that he had his own variation of that verse: "I must increase, then I must increase some more."

Any real glimpse at the person, character and reality of Jesus Christ can do nothing but overwhelm the believer with an understanding of his or her TOTAL dependence on Christ. I have said often, that when we all come face to face with God at the end of our lives on earth, it is my firm belief that we will have two principal thoughts. The first will be: "I HAVE GREATLY UNDERSTIMATED THE HOLINESS OF GOD." The second will be, "I have greatly overestimated my own righteousness."

I know that the only thing that I can do on my own is the same thing I did in the ski race described above: fall on my face in disgrace and humiliation. The Apostle Paul spoke of his many credentials and accomplishments in the world, only to say, *"I count them but dung, that I may win Christ."* There is nothing wrong with having a legacy of accomplishments attained through hard work and persistent dedication to a goal, but the loftiest of accomplishments are meaningless and often even contemptuous compared to what even the seemingly most insignificant of believers can accomplish in union with Christ. This has been the great failing of the Independent Fundamental Baptist Movement in my lifetime. We trumpet in powerful oratory the manhood and bravado of the Old Testament prophets and seek to convince others how much like them we are. Then we completely forget the praise that God had for the penitent sinner in the temple who followed the Pharisee's boastings with the simple phrase: ***"God be merciful to me a sinner."*** Had Jack Hyles or Jack Schaap ever really gotten hold of the reality of that expression in their hearts, they would have left the world a far different legacy. Had they been aware that their strength comes only from God and not from their position, their church, their followers, their sycophantic preaching, or the size of the crowds they draw, we would be telling a different story about them today. Their cadre of abuse victims would lovingly remember their birthdays today like we do those of our own family.

These men had enormous talent, ambition, vision and confidence. It is not a very common occurrence in history when these assets are found in one individual. The problem is that those assets can eventually become severe liabilities if we do not acknowledge their source or use them in the way they were intended. David declined the use of Saul's sword and armor to fight the giant Goliath. He knew that he could not wield them effectively and chose instead a humble weapon that today is a child's toy: a slingshot. With that inauspicious device he slew a giant and established a fame that has lasted 3,100 years. Jack Schaap made a different choice. When Jack Hyles handed him a massive sword and a suit of armor that fit him like the gunbelt Hyles had given him on the occasion of his thirtieth birthday, he saw only the glory he thought could be his. He lost sight of the fact that they presented a risk even beyond the scope of that glory. In August of 2012, that sword slipped from his hand and that very symbol of power pierced his heart.

It is hard to imagine or do justice to the good someone like Jack Schaap could have done. Sadly, he believed the praises and adulation that the fawning crowds laid weekly at his feet. Instead of the mantra of John the Baptist, ***"He must increase and I must decrease,"*** he chose the mantra of a young Louisville boxer once named Casius Clay: **"I am the greatest!"** He elevated himself weekly from the pulpit beyond what should have been tolerable for any Christian to hear. When the fawning crowds that surrounded Jesus tried to make Him king, Jesus ran in the other direction:

"When Jesus therefore perceived that they would come and take him by force, to make him a king, he departed again into a mountain himself alone."
John 6:15

Jack Schaap responded by saying, "the line forms here." Jack Schaap welcomed the adulation and glory of that congregation. In fact, he reveled in it because he thought he was worthy. His glory, however was stolen from God. Could there be a surer sign that God would take that glory back some day and by so doing shout to the world, **"Your crown was stolen from Me, and I am taking it back!"**

Jack Schaap was vulgar beyond description in staff meetings, and profane in the pulpit beyond belief. His doctrinal deviations and fabrications from whole cloth knew no bounds. He was a law unto himself in every respect. Sadly, he never so much as caught a glimpse of the reality that the world beheld on August 7, 2012. His climb to the heights of ecclesiastical power only made for a bigger splat when he came crashing down before the entire nation in an avalanche of shame and humiliation with massive collateral damage to the cause of Christ that will continue for a generation, and probably well beyond.

The Bible is plain: *"There is no temptation taken you, but such as is common to man."* I am not going to say for one second that what happened to Jack Schaap in the Summer of 2012 could never happen to me. I may perhaps be safe in saying that it would be unlikely that it could happen overnight. There must be a progression of desensitizing practices and events, I believe, that lead a Christian in that direction. We can all get to the place where sin is no longer *"exceedingly sinful."* In a nutshell, it happens when our lives are immersed in the world and not daily in the Spirit of God. I think it is safe to say that such a great decline probably can take place with greater facility and at a greater pace today than in times past. <u>I believe that for a man to be obsessed with things sexual to the point that they permeate his life, charge every conversation and his every thought, pornography must surely be the fuel of such a perverse appetite.</u>

I have no doubt that this had a lot to do with Jack Schaap sexualizing so much of what he preached and taught to the point where he was not able to so much as see the massive and crass vulgarity of his sugarstick sermon, "A Polished Shaft." This is when Jack Schaap opened the curtain to his mind for all to see, and didn't even realize it. This was a moment of shame and degradation for the cause of Christ, and an absolute and joyous delight to the God haters and mockers in the world. Their words are recorded all over the Internet in the comments on this inglorious moment memorialized forever in Schaap's disgraceful actions from the pulpit.

If there is one thing that I know and have no qualms about expressing, it is this: THERE BUT FOR THE GRACE OF GOD GO I! Does Schaap deserve the contempt his very name will bring to mind for a generation? Yes he does. Does that mean that we have the right to ever see ourselves as beyond the scope and reach of such sins? NO!!! This may not sit well with some readers, but please allow me to expound: IT IS THAT VERY UNDERSTANDING OF HUMAN FALLIBILITY THAT HAS CAUSED ME FOR MANY YEARS TO COME TO GOD DAILY AND CONFESS MY UTTER INCAPACITY AND WEAKNESS IN THE ABSENCE OF HIS DAILY BLESSINGS ON MY LIFE!

If I can give any Christian any advice, and if that is all you get out of anything that I have to say, "Go thou and do likewise!"

For some, the hurt at the hands of the I.F.B. abusers has been so great that it has turned to bitterness and anger. I have seen this in many places, and I understand that because of that, nothing I say will be well received by those whose anger has turned into hate because I once represented this movement. If I condemn 99% of it, that will not be enough for some. They will see my efforts as just another sermon— just more preaching. All I can say to those people, is that I will pray for you. Jesus, not religion has a way out of the wilderness for you and back to His side. I hope you find it. Much of the reason for writing this book is to put in place markers directing the way to that recovery while bypassing the crags and cliffs of anger and bitterness, as well as false religion.

If your days do not begin by having this kind of confession of your human frailty to God, then my friend, you are on the Jack Schaap road. Look closely and you will see the footprints of Jack Hyles, Jimmy Swaggart, Jim Baker, Dave Hyles, and a host of other disgraced Christian leaders who stood in the starting gate and smugly proclaimed, "<u>I don't fall</u>." Yes you do fall. Your fall may very well be around the next corner. It is called being human. There is only one Man who never fell, and He has scars in His hands that He suffered in catching me when I fell.

The night before every ski race, I went to the workbench with my skis and my toolbox, often staying late into the evening. In some hotels, I could hear the rock beat of the nightclub near the ski room. While admittedly drawn to the good times my friends were having meeting beautiful people from all over the world, I would work away at an old wooden, wax covered workbench filing the edges of my skis as sharp as I could get them. I scraped the bottoms flat with an instrument I had made in a machine shop that was true to a few thousandths of an inch so I could make sure my ski bases were flat and true. I waxed my skis to make them fast

23

and as smooth as they could be in the turns. I studied the physics of skiing everywhere I could find someone willing to share with me what they knew. I never relied on raw talent, probably because I didn't have all that much of it; this fact was painfully driven home for me after my first racing season in Europe. Though pitted weekly against great talent, I relied on preparation and a determination to never, ever fail for lack of effort, or commitment. Years later I brought that spirit into my Christian life, and it has served me well. It is the spirit expressed by Jacob as he wrestled with the angel:

"I will not let thee go unless thou bless me."
Genesis 3:26

Jack Schaap had enormous talent. He had learned from his predecessor that Christians would flock in droves to hear a man whose thundering tones made them think of the great preachers of the Bible: Isaiah, Jeremiah, Moses, Ezekiel, John the Baptist, Paul and others. Unfortunately, none of us were able, or perhaps willing, to see past the performance and try to morally validate the man delivering the messages. We had completely forgotten that Jesus was once described as having *"a meek and quiet spirit."* We had forgotten that when a man has a genuine encounter with Jesus Christ, he does what John did on Patmos: *"I fell on my face as dead."* We forgot that Isaiah's reaction to the presence of God was to see himself for what he really was and cry out to God: *"Woe is me, for I am a man of unclean lips!"* These great men did not rush back to their pulpits and deliver an oration with over 300 self references and only five to God, as I had once personally observed Jack Hyles do. They were not all about what was wrong, weak, inferior, or cowardly about other men. They were all about their own shortcomings as they cried out to God for redemption, for mercy and for forgiveness.

Why did it take me six years to see this? Were the Bible passages expressing the virtue of humility, the foolishness of self-sufficiency, and the abomination of personal pride obscure passages that only a great theologian could understand? Of course not! It should have been evident to ALL of us who sat under these men's preaching that they neither embodied nor reflected the spirit of Jesus Christ. It should have been obvious that their preaching was biblically flavored at best, and not founded on a sound and balanced systematic theology. It was obvious to one ten year old boy sitting on our pew one morning in the vast auditorium of First Baptist Church of Hammond. Johnny Colsten had just finished reading the Scripture that would thematically launch the Hyles sermon to follow. After the verses were read, this little lad shut his Bible and put it in the rack next to the big maroon songbooks and looked at his father sitting next to him and said: "We won't be needing that any more this morning, will we Dad?"

That was when a light went on for me. It was not a brilliant floodlight or a piercing spotlight in the shrouded fog of darkness, but it was a light. Was this awakening the fruit of a Bible college degree in Pastoral Theology? Was it because something didn't jive with the Greek origin of a Bible text that I had studied in my two year seminary program? No. It was because a ten year old boy had understood what thousands of well meaning Christians had missed: the Bible was not going to be preached in our church that morning; a man was going to be exalted. Ultimately, any man who travels that road will fall.

"And the rain descended, and the floods came, and the winds blew and beat upon that house; and it fell: and great was the fall of it."
Matt. 7:27

25

"He was a dynamic, young, authoritative and exalted presence before a thousand college co-eds in a school where he became chancellor. He presided over the massive Youth Conferences every summer. There was every indication that he was addicted to pornography. What could possibly go wrong?"

Chapter

3

Pigs In A Blanket

It was the Fall of 1989. I felt very blessed to be a part of First Baptist Church of Hammond and to be as close as I was to the leadership. I had just graduated from their seminary and received an M.Th., a Master's degree in Pastoral Theology, a two year program. The fact that I had become a part of the "inner circle" was not nearly as relevant and meaningful to me as the fact that I had made some meaningful friendships there and that I thought I had a future there.

Among those with whom I enjoyed a meaningful friendship were Jack Hyles and Jack Schaap. I was high on Hyles' list, and it was fairly apparent to me and a number of others there that I was being groomed for a staff position in some kind of significant capacity. (I will publish a number of letters that I received from Hyles in the appendix of this book, as I am sure that there will be those lining up to refute and deny all of this. Feel free to impale yourselves on the facts provided.)

It was in that climate that attorney Voyle Glover wrote his now famous 450 page book, *"Fundamental Seduction"* in which he chronicled the abuses of Jack Hyles and his administrative cadre of willing accomplices at First Baptist Church of Hammond (the "Bobbleheads"). It is critically important for the reader to note that I did not read *Fundamental Seduction* because I had any compelling suspicion of any serious moral wrongdoing on the part of Jack Hyles. In fact, I read the book for one reason and one reason only: I wanted to be better able to defend my preacher. As one may correctly surmise, it did not turn out that way. Glover was a skilled trial lawyer with a solid understanding of biblical principles expressed in a 200,000 word book. *Fundamental Seduction* turned out to be a dagger in the heart of Jack Hyles. That book crippled his ministry. Later, the Internet would decimate his legacy.

The week after I read the book, I had a breakfast meeting with Jack Schaap to discuss our business venture. We were working on selling franchises of my truck washing business, Budget Mobile Truck Wash. We met at 'Round the Clock", a restaurant on US 30 in Merrillville, Indiana, just up the road from Hyles-Anderson College. We sat in the first booth on the left, the one closest to the door. Schaap sat with his back to the entrance and I sat across from him. He ordered Pigs in a Blanket.

Soon our food arrived. We had just begun eating when I made the following statement: "I read the book." I will never forget Schaap's reaction. I was stunned by it. He was my dear friend. He had married my wife and me. He had been in our home. We had recently been invited to a wonderful Fourth of July celebration in his home. It was a beautiful home that had obviously been decorated exclusively by a woman. I remember telling him what a lovely home he had. His only response was, "I live in a doll house."

When I spoke the words to Schaap that morning, "I read the book," Schaap had a reaction I never would have predicted in a million years. He did not so much wait until he had finished chewing his food. He grabbed his napkin, wiped his mouth, and got up and left without uttering one word! I was stunned. It became apparent to me that I had in one second gone from trusted friend, business partner, and co-laborer in the Lord's vineyard to a massive liability with whom he was entirely unwilling to be identified in any way. Our friendship was over. The door had slammed shut with such a resounding and thunderous noise that I knew it would never be reopened. I was right. It has remained closed for twenty-three years.

I have written Jack Schaap several letters since that day over a period of more than twenty years (see Appendix). I guess that in all fairness, I should not fail to acknowledge in some way the value I placed on the meaningful friendship that we had shared and the good times that we had at one time enjoyed together serving the Lord. For a long time, we drove to Purdue University in Lafayette, Indiana every Wednesday as part of an outreach ministry of the church. I had been friends with Dr. Henry Morris of the Institute for Creation Research in California and I was greatly influenced by this wonderful man. He had been close by and a regular speaker in my church in San Diego. I was able to attend a highly educational graduate seminar there. The Purdue Ministry was something that I had hoped would enable me to engage the students there in a meaningful scientific discussion on the flaws of Evolution and the scientific evidence for Creation that was beginning to emerge then.

I think that having grown up in a Christian environment, Purdue University was the first time Schaap had witnessed firsthand the aftermath of the sexual revolution that had begun in the 1960's. I would not go so far as to characterize Schaap's reaction to the lifestyle that some of the Purdue students described to him there as an obsession. I did hear him tell over and over, however, the story of a young male student who cancelled an appointment he had to speak with Schaap because there were two girls waiting for him in his dorm room for a three-way sexual liaison. He also made a reference one day to the Purdue co-eds as being clad "in fishnet with no underwear." This was something that I had certainly never seen there. I have never been able to rid myself of the suspicion that this became a stumbling block for Schaap that would never go away. If my surmisings are indeed correct, and one adds this kind of fantasy to the mix of opportunities for temptation regularly presented to Schaap, then the ensuing moral challenge can be seen as daunting for him. He was a dynamic, young, authoritative and exalted presence before a thousand college co-eds in a school where he became chancellor. He presided over the massive Youth Conferences every Summer. There was every indication that he was addicted to pornography. It would seem that the conclusion we should draw can best be summed up in a statement we have all heard before: ***"what could possibly go wrong?"***

Chapter

4

When A Man Sells His Soul

The business deal that Jack Schaap and I had put together for a franchise of my truck washing business began to go badly. I had put together a mobile wash truck with all of the equipment needed to do mobile truck washing and sold it to a man from the church. I had been washing trucks for some time while at Hyles-Anderson College and Hyles-Anderson Seminary, and it became a very successful business. This was the mid-eighties and I rarely grossed less than $75 an hour. On some accounts that figure rose to $125 an hour. I had no employees and my equipment was quickly paid for, so after deducting for fuel and chemicals, most of my income was profit. This was not lost on Jack Schaap.

I trained the man we were putting in business, and he turned the bulk of the money over to us. The agreed upon price was $25,000. We paid for the equipment and split the rest of the money evenly. Then one day as I was visiting Schaap in his office after classes as I did often, he told me that our client was not being successful in the business and wanted his money back. It turned out that the first three Saturdays he was in business he was incapable of finding the truck lots in which he had been scheduled to wash in Hammond, and

31

the customers got rid of him. We did not feel like this was our responsibility or our problem, but the situation quickly escalated when the client went to see his pastor, Jack Hyles.

Schaap told me not to worry that the guy was "dumber than a box of rocks" and he was confident that we had done everything right and that Hyles would see through it all. We all met in Hyles' office for two-and-a-half hours. I had the utmost confidence in Hyles and was not a bit worried. We had been one hundred percent honest and above board in all our dealings with this man. We had provided him with one hundred hours of training, a reliable, heavy-duty fully equipped wash truck, two 55 gallon drums of product, and $30,000 worth of good customer accounts.

At the end of all this time in Hyles' office, Hyles handed each person there a three by five card. Then he said that each of us was to write on their card the amount that we believed our client was owed. I sat in stunned silence. We had made a convincingly strong case that he was owed nothing. There was never any question of any blame assigned to Schaap and me for anything we had said or done. The man could not point to one paragraph in our contract that we had not honored. Yet now, the verdict by Hyles was that he was owed money, and the only question on the table was how much. My view was that he owed us $8,000. I put "MINUS $8,000" on my card and handed it to Hyles."

Then Hyles looked at Schaap and said the following words: *"You and Jerry owe these people all the money they paid you. You see it, don't you, Jack? You do see it, right?"* In fact Schaap had never seen it. He had for weeks been of the same opinion as I was: we didn't owe this man a dime! We both knew full well that he fell on his face all by himself. But that was not how Schaap responded to his father-in-law. He spoke the following words without a moment's hesitation: *"Oh, yes! I see it."* The whole time he was shaking his head so fast that it was almost a blur. *"Yes, I see it, Preacher. I see it!"* He looked to me like a pathetic puppy dog who had just peed on the carpet and was being scolded. He did not have a shred of manhood or character in his wimpy act of contrition and condescension that went squarely against what I knew he believed. He was a compromised man, and I would never see him in the same way again.

This was perhaps the first time that I saw the character of Jack Hyles for what it was. The figure that I had placed on the three by five card was MINUS $8,000, because that was what I believed the man owed us. He had only paid $17,000 of the agreed upon $25,000. In the many phone conversations that had taken place, I had always said the same thing to him: "Go get our signed contract and tell me which one of the provisions you believe we have violated." His answer was always the same: "The whole thing!" He had no case and Schaap and I knew it.

Now Schaap had thoroughly caved in to Hyles and did an about face when Hyles had asked him, "You see it, don't you Jack?" In fact, Schaap and I saw the very same thing: Hyles was not at all concerned with what was fair or just. He was purely advocating on behalf of the church and trying to keep from losing a tithing church member. Nothing could have been more clear to me. I knew it was just as clear to Schaap, but it was hard for him to disagree with the man to whom he had sold his soul.

In all of this, as I sat there in Jack Hyles' office, I felt as if I had been betrayed by a friend, not just my hero. He had often called me "my buddy" in letters [see appendix]. Those letters had been filled with praise and appreciation for all that I had done for him. Sadly, I believed it all. And so when I saw that this man was willing to sell me out for the sake of church politics and to dig into my pocket to the tune of many thousands of dollars, I had but one thought: "THAT IS NOT GOING TO HAPPEN!"

Was this man, Jack Schaap, the man who had thundered from the pulpit so powerfully as to be the idol of every young preacher in training at Hyles-Anderson College? Was this the man who could preach to vast crowds with or without a microphone? Was this the rock star homiletics professor who taught us how to project power and authority from the pulpit in a way that few had ever seen in our generation? No, this was a different man. It was a man who had sold his soul and his manhood. I had just been witness to one of the payments being delivered. My trusted and admired friend Jack Schaap had just sold his dignity for the privilege of remaining the heir-apparent to the throne of Jack Hyles.

"A good name is rather to be chosen than great riches, and loving favour rather than silver and gold."
Proverbs 22:22

Chapter

5

Living In A Cult Church

One Sunday morning before Sunday School as I was wandering around the auditorium at First Baptist Church of Hammond before Jack Hyles' auditorium Sunday School class, I noticed that a friend of mine was not in his usual seat. In the row behind him was a Hyles Anderson College staff member. I shook his hand and asked him where the missing brother was. His smile gave way to a very serious look. As he leaned forward and lowered his tone, he replied: *"so-and-so developed a critical spirit."* At that point in my life, the scales had not yet fallen, although there were signs that they would be falling before too terribly long. I did not react, but I filed that statement away for later analysis. I knew that something was not right.

Implicit in this man's assessment of why the man in the pew in front of his had left was that it was not a good thing to ever express criticism or dissent. There was no room for this practice at First Baptist Church of Hammond. Hyles was ways fond of saying. *"I will always be a friend to my friends."* This was a bald faced lie. What he should have added was that the condition for his friendship was that you never disagreed with him, publicly or privately. Why? Because cults do not tolerate dissent.

35

For cults, the operative word is control. There can be no complete control without complete agreement. A college staff member once stood up in Hyles' "Six o'clock Question and Answer Time" held each Sunday and prefaced a question he had with, "Brother Hyles, tell me what to believe about. . . ." Everyone got a good chuckle out of this, including Hyles. The problem was, as some were just beginning to realize, God was not laughing.

Christians are commanded to *"Study to shew thyself approved unto God."* We are to follow the example of the Bereans, who in Acts 17:11 were *"... more noble than those in Thessalonica, in that they. . . searched the scriptures daily, whether those things were so."* This passage was not in Hyles' repertoire. He wanted to be in charge of what you believed. The biblical doctrine of the Priesthood of the Believer did not extend far enough at First Baptist Church of Hammond for Hyles to even begin thinking about accommodating even the slightest deviation or alternate interpretation in doctrine or even style or emphasis among his followers. Hyles even went so far as to coin the term, BLIND LOYALTY." Never did I hear him present a biblical defense for it, but it was as big a buzzword as ever went around that church.

People were measured, hired, fired, promoted, praised, and at times publicly annihilated on the basis of their willingness or lack thereof to forget that there was only one Man who never sinned, and He lived in Nazareth two thousand years ago, not in Hammond in 1989. Sadly, I was among those people in the 1980's who believed that. In fact, I was the one who went to a button maker on Clark Street in Gary, Indiana and had a thousand of the now famous *"Hyles 100% Support"* buttons made. I sold them in the church for $2 apiece and soon had to have more made. Everyone and their brother has accused Hyles of having these made, but in all fairness I have to confess: it was me.[see Appendix]

Hyles' control was overwhelming and pervasive. It would cover all aspects of the church members' lives: how they dressed, how often they came to church, how much of their time they offered the church through its many ministries, whether or not to accept a promotion if it meant moving away from the church, where one's children attended school, how long a man's hair was, how long a woman's hair was, how long ladies' dresses should be, where church members went on vacation, whom they voted for, and on and on. It was not at all uncommon for church members to willingly extend the control Hyles maintained over their lives by waiting months for a counseling appointment to ask Hyles' advice on such menial aspects of life as what kind of used car to buy. Little children were trained early on to slip Hyles' favorite candy bar, Reeses Peanut Butter Cup under his door as a token of their devotion to "God's man."

Fear of rejection by "God's man" was the driving force that fostered complete obedience and unquestioned loyalty. Critical thinking was always discouraged, as it was seen as the expression of pride. Never mind that the greatest expression of pride in a pulpit in the twentieth century was the man they heard preach three times a week.

Everyone hoped, dreamed and fantasized that one day they would be the subject of public praise from Hyles' own lips from that pulpit. If "blind loyalty" was the price exacted, there was never any shortage of people willing to fall all over each other to claw their way to the head of that line to place their sacrifice on the Hyles altar. The slightest questioning of Hyles' authority was unthinkable and treated as rebellion worthy of ostracizing or excommunication. Families were often split right down the middle over this and many never recovered. Criticism of leadership was a career-ending move at First Baptist Church of Hammond, and Hyles would do everything he could to see to that.

Hyles' micromanagement of his people's lives extended even to the arranging of marriages. He once told a beautiful young woman on the college staff that it was God's will for her to marry a young man stricken with a debilitating disability. Hyles loved to play God that way. The problem was that the young woman did not love this young man. Marry they did, however. Eventually she left him. The distraught and despondent man took his own life. He was loved and admired throughout the college, yet not one person was courageous enough to express publicly that his blood was dripping from the hands of Jack Hyles.

One Sunday morning in the dead of winter, I was making my way to one of the back entrances of the church auditorium. In front of me was a woman who belonged to a group of wives I had come to call "bus widows." Her husband had left home in the early hours of the morning when it was still dark on a cold Chicago winter morning and driven to a Chicago bus garage to drive one of the one hundred buses the church leased every Sunday. These would then be filled with kids from the poorest of Chicago's neighborhoods, and that with or without parental permission. On a "Big day" that number doubled to two hundred buses. I knew her husband and had worked with him driving one of those buses on one of the bus routes.

She was carrying a small child and laboriously dragging two more little ones behind her in that alley filled with deep icy ruts and unplowed snow as the cold wind blew down this canyon of old brick buildings. (They were just bus workers, so their entrance was the last to be cleared after a snowstorm.) My wife and I asked her if she was OK and if we could be of any help. Beaming from ear to ear, she turned to us and said, "No, I love serving the man of God (her husband) when he is out serving God. I shined his shoes last night and told him I was so privileged to be his wife."

Some of those bus kids stayed. They were a tiny, tiny minority, but given the thousands of them that came on the buses, enough did stay to start a "bus kid high school," Hammond Baptist High School.

I personally raised money for them one year by collecting day old baked goods from local grocery stores and giving them out every Saturday at Fishermen's Club for donations. That money went to establishing a tuition scholarship at Hyles-Anderson College for one of the more promising bus kids. Later I would realize that many of these bus kids knew full well of the legacy of men like Dave Hyles. Undoubtedly they also had to know of others their age who came off those buses and were sexually abused by the only people in their young lives that they had ever associated with the righteousness of Jesus Christ. That angered and disgusted me so that I eventually found peace only in turning it all over to the Lord, whom I knew was not only far more offended than I was, but also far better able to bring about justice.

In later days, I would ask myself where the Bible says it is permissible to overturn God's directive to provide for one's own, and that those who fail in that responsibility are *"worse than infidels."* (1 Timothy 5:8) How well do I recall one such young wife whose husband placed at risk everything he held dear in life and soon became a victim of the manipulative efforts of men who cared only about publishing the church's attendance figures in The Sword of the Lord. His wife committed adultery with one of Hyles' "Bobbleheads."

Ironically, what neither this young mother of five nor her overworked husband knew was that the man who was then heading another church ministry in which her husband slavishly worked would later seduce her in a California motel room while on a preaching trip. She had been visiting friends there. This adulterous affair cost my friend his marriage and his family. They have never recovered. Hyles' response was to relocate the adulterous preacher to a church in East Texas. He was thrown out of that church for the same reason, and is now continuing in his adulterous ways as the pastor of another church in another state.

Chapter

6

The Holiness Of God

What is the holiness of God? Any attempt to wrap our human minds around this concept brings us first to an understanding that holiness is closely related to purity. By holiness we must always understand that God is separate from sin and evil. Holiness is far more than an attribute of God; it is who God is. God does not take on holiness, for if He did, there would be implied a source of holiness above God. The term "holiness" can only exist for the same reason a term like "clean" can exist. In a sterile and perfectly pure world, the word clean would not have the context necessary to its meaning. Clean only has meaning in a world where there is dirt. Likewise, holiness only has meaning in understanding how God is different from man.

We may well say that God's holiness is the overriding theme of the Old Testament and that for which God most wanted to be known. This is the principal avenue through which man can understand his relationship to God and not only how man is different from God, but also how different he is from God. The history of God's dealing with the human race is the history of God's offense at His children intertwining their lives with that which was profane or common and failing to

41

heed God's command to be separate from those influences and practices.

Depravity, that great tendency in all of us that keeps us from manifesting, embodying and reflecting the holiness of God as we were designed to do, is what provides the necessary context in which holiness can be properly understood by man. Holiness is the separation from the dirt of life. Religion is the codified process and movement on that path. It leads us to become increasingly separate from sin through an imperfect and supremely challenging effort.

Man's efforts to be holy are supported by the methodology and inspiration of Scripture, the partnership and power achieved with God through prayer, and the opportunities for self evaluation and correction provided by a good church under balanced leadership. No man can turn away from his depraved lower nature in his own strength. To *"repent with godly sorrow"* requires that all these spiritual assets be working properly and in perfect harmony. The person in this position will understand well his place in the universe, his purpose in life, and will be at peace within. It all has to begin by understanding the holiness of God and our lowly human stature by comparison.

Enter Jack Schaap. Those of us who knew him and had not thoroughly prostituted the reality of a holy God that I have made a feeble, human attempt to present here, will perhaps begin to understand the magnitude of Jack Schaap's moral failure. The moral failure of any man who sinks to the depraved level of seducing a child young enough to be his granddaughter is heinous enough in our culture to legally deprive that man of the privilege of living in our towns and neighborhoods. But Schaap's moral failures are so far beyond this level of legal transgression as to defy the understanding of God's people. The Bible teaches that *"To whom much is given, much shall be required."* Only on the basis of this applied principle can we understand the magnitude of Schaap's failure. To minimize Schaap's sin is to insult a holy God.

Jack Schaap had been a private student of Jack Hyles for many years. Hyles was his mentor. Schaap was not at all exempt from Hyles' hard and fast requirement to be venerated and lauded by those under him. I saw that first-hand. Everyone on Hyles' staff was regularly subjected publicly to what for most people would be a humiliating and demeaning level of public abasement and subjugation. Hyles had a great, great need to use others as a tool for self aggrandizement. This need went back to his childhood and his issues of abandonment attributable to his father. (I will offer a clinical diagnosis in the appendix that will, for those who knew him, be stunning in its accuracy.)

Jack Schaap understood what we all understood in that day: the road to recognition, promotion, career, stature and the opportunities for Christian service went through Jack Hyles' office door, and you had better not come empty handed! That is why life at First Baptist Church was what some would now view as a competition to exalt the man. We all brought our hopefully unblemished and highly polished offerings to his altar at every opportunity. They were the fuel for career advancement, and so much more.

There was a man there named Joe Combs. Joe Combs was the favorite Bible teacher at Hyles Anderson College, and we all heard him once say that he had to catch himself on several occasions when he began to pray and mistakenly started his prayer with,"Dear Brother Hyles." Joe Combs will have many years to contemplate the inexpressible offense that this sentiment represents to a holy God who has said that He is a jealous God who would never share His glory with another. In fact Combs has the rest of his life in a Tennessee prison to do just that after being convicted of unspeakable crimes and abuses in victimizing in unimaginable ways his adopted daughter.

I would like to sound a warning here. It is primarily for my own benefit, but I will share it with you, the reader. In all of this sort of assessment of another person, we walk the edge of a precipice, and that edge is crumbling and dangerous. We have to guard vigilantly our human tendency to declare, *"I thank God that I am not as other men,"* even when that other man is someone like Jack Schaap. In fact, each and every one of us has the potential to be just like any other man, including just like Jack Schaap.

Who is to say that if you or I were the subject of human exaltation, and veneration— some would say hero worship such as was directed to the pulpit of First Baptist Church of Hammond for half a century— that we too would not take full advantage as did Jack Schaap and Jack Hyles? Who is to say that we would immediately deflect those praises and adulations upward to Christ when the package in which they came was addressed to us? Far better to maintain a most humble and lowly profile than to face that temptation. The pages of history are full of men who failed to redirect those packages to their rightful recipient.

For my inoculation against this disease of pride, imperfect though any vaccine may be, and to see an example of a properly founded perspective on humanity, I always turn to Job. I have thought and studied Job much in my Christian life, culminating in a short book—my biographical sketch of Job as part of a series entitled, *"Heroes of the Valley."*

We have it from God himself that Job was the human being on earth who most impressed God. Job had blessings untold from God, attracting even the eye of Satan. Job had a national reputation for his character, wisdom, wealth and godliness. Yet even a man such as Job knew the implications for him of the holiness of God. Even in his own comparatively profane human level of servitude, Job understood who he was relative to a holy and sovereign God. Job was painfully aware, even in his inexpressible and unprecedented pall of misery and anguish, that he was being presumptuous and out of line in even daring to address God about his tragic life:

"Behold, I am vile; what shall I answer thee?
I will lay mine hand upon my mouth."
Job 40:3

In my three decades as a Christian, I honestly cannot think of a more diametrically opposed expression of Job's humble sentiment and understanding of what he was compared to a holy God than the tidal wave of pride and self-exaltation that has flowed from the pulpit of First Baptist Church of Hammond for fifty-three years. One can only marvel at the supernatural patience of God—at the hundreds and perhaps thousands of warnings that had come from those who were once close to Hyles and Schaap (as close as anyone could be to narcissists of this magnitude). These were men who had the courage and vision to speak out. Sadly, however, these brave Christians like Voyle Glover, Vick Nischik, George Godfrey and Robert Sumner could not overcome the influence of Hyles' and Schaap's enablers: the "men" on the platform, the teachers in the classrooms and the leaders of Fundamentalism who continued right up until the end to invite Schaap to highlight their conferences and legitimize their own positions of leadership in the I.F.B. Movement.

I can only shudder and sometimes even weep at the effect this must have had on so many of the victims who were treated as criminals and selfish offenders who "raised their hands against God's anointed" and in so doing were accused of damaging a movement that God had ordained for the salvation of a nation. These thoughts bring me to a sometimes bewildering position of awe at God's restraint, patience and the supremacy of His desire to always offer an avenue of redemption right up to the moment when the ground opens and swallows that which is evil. The warnings given to Jack Schaap abounded right up to the end.

Sometimes I like to ask people, "Other than Jesus, with what Bible character would you like to spend an afternoon?" The responses are always interesting to me, and certainly make for some interesting and imaginative conversations. One of the great delights in writing my book about Heaven, *"The Bench—A Heavenly Conversation,"* was that I was able through the literary license of fiction to bring some of those encounters to life. Though fictional, this book rests on a solid biblical foundation, particularly with respect to the science.

I have often thought that I would like to meet one of the Old Testament High Priests. I say this because they, of all people, had a dedication to spiritual purity. They knew that they had to exude all the holiness possible for a human being, and then some, to survive their yearly sojourn into the Holy of Holies as they brought the sacrifice before a holy God. This personal holiness of theirs had to come from the core of their being. It was not something added on. It was who they were.

This is especially important because the awareness of holiness for an Old Testament high priest or anyone else for that matter can properly come only from having understood the reality of God's holiness. The Pharisees (and their many modern day counterparts) systematized and quantified the process of faking that holiness. Their standard was everyone around them, hence the key biblical phrase that has symbolized their self-image for 2,000 years: *"I thank God that I am not as other men."*

The reality of personal and divine holiness that lived in the soul of every high priest was a completely foreign concept to Jack Schaap and Jack Hyles, and to all the Fundamentalist

John Waynes of the I.F.B. world. Their manifestation of the pharisaical catch phrase in the preceding paragraph and the sentiment they manifested to God was the diametric opposite of the trembling High Priest. The High Priest, having done all to purify body, mind and soul, still walked into the Holy of Holies with bells sewn to the fringe of his garments and a rope around his ankle. The purpose of the bells was to give notice by their silence should he not survive the power and brilliance of God's presence. The rope was to pull him out before what remained of him was then consumed by the blinding fire of God's holiness.

This is the presence that blinded the Apostle Paul on the Damascus Road. This is the holy fire that consumed the burning bush and whose glow remained on Moses' face enough to frighten those who later looked upon him. This was the brilliance that sent John face first into the earth of Patmos when he beheld it. This was the holy brilliance that led Isaiah to self-condemnation as he saw himself as *"a man of unclean lips."* This was the part of God that Jack Schaap and Jack Hyles never, ever grasped, and certainly never embodied or reflected.

A lady who was once our neighbor when we lived in Northwest Indiana told us the story of when she confronted Jack Hyles' infamous son Dave Hyles about his serial adultery. She was a teacher in one of the schools of First Baptist Church of Hammond. Dave Hyles had an integral part in the ministries of First Baptist Church of Hammond. Dave Hyles' philanderings were well known even by those whose heads were deeply buried in the sands of hero worship. It was well known by the thousands of people whose regular job it was to hold up the edges of the rug so the scandal sweepers could regularly ply their despicable craft and pay their dues to their god, Jack Hyles.

Dave Hyles did not hesitate for a second and gave this answer to the inquiring woman: "GREAT MEN HAVE

GREAT NEEDS!" Why God allows a despicable miscreant like Dave Hyles to breathe His air one second beyond having uttered this incomprehensible abomination is a mystery that will have to await the divine perspective of Heaven for me to understand. Even if I wrote a separate book on it, there is no earthly way to encompass in mere words all that is wrong and vile about a phrase such as this.

When Dave Hyles returned from having devastated two churches to which his father had sent him, much in the same manner as Catholic Bishops reshuffle pedophile priests, First Baptist Church of Hammond gave him a standing ovation! I was there. His sister Linda Murphrey numbers the affairs Dave had in those churches at over thirty-five. Jack and Cindy Schaap were sitting about a dozen rows behind us and one section to our left, about three rows in front of one of the exits. I immediately turned to see if they were standing and applauding Dave. THEY WERE! My heart sank.

So what is it then that draws Christians to men like Hyles and Schaap? One day it just hit me. This was my epiphany of understanding that for me bridged the chasm. I am speaking of the great gulf fixed between the confusion and perplexity that so many Christians experience when they hear the litany of abuses at the hands of the two Jacks, and the obvious dichotomy these two evidenced with the principles and character of Jesus Christ.

Hyles and Schaap appealed far more to men than to women. Herein lies the mystery to the riddle of how they can claim to represent a holy God. Many men crave a voice to cry out against hypocrisy and injustice in this world. This has to do more with social tenets and philosophies than it does the attributes of Christ. Men are drawn to any powerful man who can rail and thunder against organizations like the A.C.L.U., the National Organization for Women, the National Education Association, P.E.T.A., Save the Whales,

Greenpeace, homosexual advocacy groups, and on and on the list goes.

Jack Hyles learned how to champion the social conservative causes, and he did it under the banner of religion while waving a King James Bible in one hand and shaking his other fist menacingly in the air. I can still visualize his facial contortions during those thundering rants.

Understandably, the men who were drawn to him did not want to hear of Jesus' "meek and quiet spirit." They wanted powerful denunciations of everything in their world that made them mad and left them feeling impotent and wronged. **Hyles and Schaap became their source of social-spiritual testosterone.** They were the reincarnation of the Old Testament prophets, but they lacked the ability and the propensity to weave into those doctrines anything having to do with the holiness or grace of a loving God.

"So will I make my holy name known in the midst of my people Israel; and I will not let them pollute my holy name any more."
Ezekiel 39:7

"It took me a long time to control the fizz in my pop bottle of religious idealism. Maybe that is because I allowed others to shake it three times a week for so many years. Maybe it was because the fizz tickled my palate. In the end, the bottle went flat, the mold grew, and my stomach hurt."

Chapter

7

I'll Never Go To Church Again

If I went with my first reaction in dealing with this subject, this would be a very short chapter. In fact, it would consist of four words: "I don't blame you." I have seen far more of the seamy underbelly of the Independent Fundamental Baptist Movement than I have of its nobility and virtue—<u>FAR more</u>!

However, I want to accomplish two things here: I want to help people who have chucked church altogether, and I want to tap into the mind of God to understand the purpose of the church. I want to focus on God's thoughts on what the relationship of the church ought to be to the Christian, your personal experience with the church or mine notwithstanding. That is not all that a easy task for me to undertake. I have seen too much in church that makes a balanced approach a formidable challenge for me. My gut tells me that there may well not be a significant redeeming value in the Independent Fundamental Baptist Movement, save the rare decent church out there in a vast wasteland. But, I want to wipe the fog of personal cynicism off my windshield, turn the headlights on bright, and try to pierce the brown acid smog of anger, resentment, disappointment, hurt, and even the unbridled hatred that so many feel toward these churches, often including me.

I understand all of those feelings. I would never so much as imply to anyone that those feelings are inappropriate, misguided, or misplaced. In the end, however, I have never been able to blame God, nor have I been tempted to. If I were to paraphrase God's response to Job's minuscule foray into that landscape, I would bring out my best Brooklyn accent and characterize God as saying to Job: *"Hey . . . Are you talkin' to ME?"*

First of all, we should never lose sight of the fact that the church is not the modern day tabernacle in the wilderness, or the Old Testament Temple. I think it is ill-advised to call a church "God's house." This does not reflect an accurate view of the New Testament church's foundation or of how it was designed to function. The church, though divinely appointed, is a human institution. It is where religion is practiced. Religion is the presentation of God's person, God's purpose, God's Law and God's future entrusted into the hands of failure-prone men. Those things are entrusted to human beings, and human beings can be counted on to do one thing consistently: to fall short.

The New Testament Church was never intended as the principal place where Christians go to meet God. That is the province and personal responsibility of the individual believer in the privacy of his or her prayer closet, and within the pages of Scripture. Jesus' very name is synonymous with these Scriptures, NOT with the church. A great deal of our disappointment with churches stems from the fact that we expect far too much from them given their human administration and necessary hierarchy. I don't know if anyone has been more guilty of this than have I. It took me a long time to control the fizz in my pop bottle of idealism. Maybe that is because I allowed others to shake it for me three times a week for so many years. Maybe it was because the fizz tickled my palate. In the end, the bottle went flat, the mold grew, and my stomach hurt. Jack Schaap and Jack

Hyles were among the greatest practitioners in the history of the Independent Fundamental Baptist Church movement in the art of shaking that pop bottle. Man, were they good at it!

The church of the first century was a simple band of believers who held a common bond of worship, love, and fellowship. The most important element of this church, a "called out assembly," was the INTERPERSONAL relationship that these early believers enjoyed based on their common veneration of Jesus Christ. Paul gives us some important foundational principles concerning the church, and he places a great deal of emphasis very early on upon this "horizontal" principle detailing the church's function:

> *"And let us consider one another to provoke unto love and to good works."*
> Hebrews 10:24

This horizontal concept of assembly is the polar opposite of the centralization of power, the mechanism and foundation of all systematic control and abuse in any organization. This has nothing to do with the later extrabiblical church hierarchy that was imposed largely through human efforts to achieve human goals through a centralization of power, which is ALWAYS the enemy of freedom and liberty. It was the influence of Augustine along these very lines that led to the birth of the Roman Catholic Church. The driving force there was the VERY OPPOSITE of what believers are commanded to practice as a church.

The Roman Catholic Church was all about one thing: the CENTRALIZATION OF POWER. This is a "vertical" church polity. Paul was describing a HORIZONTAL church dynamic in Hebrews. Hyles and Schaap went in the other direction with the pedal to the metal. Soon the engine redlined, and the wall came closer on every turn until wheels and sheet metal went flying and there was massive injury in the stands as the track was strewn with car parts, and the stands with bleeding victims.

The horizontal church dynamic is important on another level as well. Apart from the vertical hierarchy and management (polity) in many churches, there is also quite often a "pulpit-down" flow. Certainly this cannot be criticized per-se. That being said, however, it must be understood in terms of how it limits the horizontal dynamic, divinely designed into the New Testament Church.

I often say that I have been in two genuine revivals. If you have to ask yourself if you have ever been in one, I can assure you of one thing: YOU HAVE NOT! This would be like asking a man fishing on a high railroad trestle just a few inches wider than the trains that cross it if he had seen a freight train come across the trestle at one hundred miles per hour. I can guarantee you that if he has to think about it, he has not seen a train.

Both genuine revivals that I have been in had three things in common:

- They both happened spontaneously independently of the preaching.
- They can both be described only as, "like standing under Niagara Falls."
- They were both started by women sitting in the pews.

In other words, these revivals involved far more of a "HORIZONTAL" church dynamic than the more vertical pulpit-to-congregation pattern. This is certainly not to imply anything negative about preaching. It is to say, however, that the only two revivals that I have been in happened when the preacher had the sensitivity to the Spirit of God to understand that God wants to at times move through the people in the congregation, not just the man behind the pulpit. In one of those two revivals, there were over 300 people at the altar crying out to God and confessing their sins and begging for divine mercy. That lasted for close to an hour. There were perhaps six or seven people left in the pews, and that may have been because the crowd at the altar was ten or twelve deep across the entire front of the church and there was no more room.

In the other revival described in my book on churches, *Clouds Without Rain*, one woman came forward after I had preached. She was trembling and weeping as she took my hand and said to me, *"Dr. Jerry, I don't want my church to die."* Her church was on the verge of fading into oblivion, and she had the honesty to say it. As I knelt with her to pray, I felt the presence of God in a way that can only be described as paralyzing. I was literally overwhelmed. I stood up to speak after we prayed, and I could not speak. My vocal chords would not work. I am not exaggerating. I tried to explain in vain what was going on. Fortunately I didn't have to explain to anyone. They knew. That church too emptied out upon the altar and poured their hearts out to God. This was a revival, not a church service.

If you would today ask anyone in either one of those church events if there had been revival, I can guarantee you one thing: nobody would say, "I think so." They would undoubtedly be far wiser than I in understanding that they could not describe it, and they would not even try. The old time evangelists when they got together would only ask one question of each other when they heard of a revival being held by one of their brethren: referring to the Holy Spirit, they would simply ask, **"Did it break through?"** The answer was either "yes" or "no." For me, it "broke through" twice. Both times the breakthrough started in the pews, not the pulpit. Both times the revival began with a woman.

This would no doubt be a good time to closely examine another verse in Hebrews, for it is one of the most commonly misunderstood verses in the church today. In particular, many Independent Fundamental Baptist pastors have become adept at promoting and teaching a false interpretation of this verse to solidify their authority over the church. Most of them do it through ignorance rather than malevolence. <u>NEITHER ONE IS EXCUSABLE</u>! I am speaking of Hebrews 13:17.

"Obey them that have the rule over you, and submit yourselves."

The truth is that I have met very few Christians who understand what this verse truly means. I have met hundreds of pastors who believe that they should be obeyed unconditionally by church members. This is not AT ALL what this verse teaches!

Let us first look at the heart of this verse, the verb "obey." There are verbs in the Bible that have a type of military connotation or directive. These are most always in the IMPERATIVE tense. They are akin to an authoritative military command that must be obeyed. This is not at all the grammatical underpinning of the verb "obey" in this verse. The verb is presented in the PRESENT tense, not the imperative tense. There is a substantial difference.

But there is something far more important going on here, and it has to do with the core meaning of the word "obey" itself. The word in the manuscripts from which our Bible derives is the Greek word *"peitho."* So what does this word normally convey? Is it the kind of command that a drill instructor would give a military recruit in a training exercise? Hardly! The word itself derives from the same word that the New Testament writers used hundreds of times for FAITH: *"episteuo."* If there is a recognized authority in the Christian world on the meaning of Greek New Testament words it is Vine. In his unabridged *"Expository Dictionary of New Testament Words"* on page 806, Vine gives the following definition for the word "obey" found in Hebrews 13:17:

"The obedience suggested is not by submission to authority, but resulting from persuasion."

If there is one verse in the Bible that more I.F.B. pastors have violated in practice, spirit and substance, I cannot think of one to whom more damage has been inflicted than Hebrews 13:17. This verse has been violently pried loose from its proper textual underpinning and twisted, tortured, prostituted and body-slammed into unconsciousness in many, many I.F.B. churches. The KING of these abusers and the one who anointed himself to lead that charge in Fundamentalism was JACK HYLES. His protegé JACK SCHAAP took up the cause in lock step with his mentor father-in-law without missing a beat when Hyles passed away in 2001. This is always made easier when Christians are unwilling to accept the responsibilities that are inherently conveyed to them in the biblical doctrine of the Priesthood of the Believer.

We tend to find comfort in having a king appointed over us to tell us what is right and wrong, as was the case in the days of King Saul. We do not understand the implications of the temple veil being rent FROM TOP TO BOTTOM when Christ died on the cross. After that, YOU became the Holy Place and Jesus is the High Priest, NOT YOUR PASTOR!

Unfortunately, every aspiring child cowboy needs a John Wayne, and every believer unwilling to "study to show thyself approved unto God" needs a spiritual John Wayne in the pulpit of his or her church, complete with the stereotypical swagger of the Fundamentalist pulpiteers. This opens the door wide to impostors and abusers. They never seem to have to kick that door in; we open it for them, and they regularly supply us with the large nails that we gladly use to nail it in that position.

This is precisely what happened when the elders of Israel came to Samuel in Ramah, and said:

*"Behold, thou art old, and thy sons walk not in thy
ways: now make us a king to judge us like all
the nations."*
I Samuel 8:5

*"But the thing displeased Samuel,
when they said, Give us a king to judge us."*
I Samuel 8:6

The truth is that Jack Hyles and Jack Schaap were the
farthest thing imaginable from biblical preachers. Hyles
mocked expository preaching (verse-by-verse) often. I heard
him say that expository preaching, or preaching through the
Bible was like going to a pharmacy and starting on one shelf
and taking medicine and working your way through every
shelf. I think back to the time when I heard him say that
from the pulpit and I become very upset with myself for
not standing up and shouting at the top of my lungs: **"ARE
YOU NUTS!?"** I say this because what Hyles was in fact
saying was that the Bible is filled with many things that can
hurt you badly. The only safe way to proceed, according to
Hyles' premise, is to be spoon fed by your preacher who in
his unchallengeable wisdom knows what you need, when you
need it, how much of it you need, and will always tell you just
how to apply it in your life. For the record, that application
at First Baptist Church of Hammond will have something to
do with exalting him and building up the church. You can bet
on that.

Expository preaching is what I call "keeping a short leash"
to the Bible. Hyles was a devotional preacher. His messages
were biblical only in a thematic sense. He never consistently
put chunks of biblical meat on anyone's plate. He sprinkled
artificial meat flavor on things he had concocted and he
became a master at disguising those concoction as meat.

Schaap learned that methodology ever so well. In fact, he
took more liberties with doctrine than anyone had imagined

he ever would, even by Hyles' malleable standards. Knowing Schaap as well as I did, I believe that I can offer a good reason for this: Schaap cultivated his depravity to the point where it took over his mind almost completely. There is no other earthly explanation for his inexpressibly vulgar sermon, "A Polished Shaft." This sermon has now become the object of a new level of derision and ridicule nationwide on YouTube. (It is so graphically vulgar that you will not want to watch it in mixed company and will probably be so disturbed by it as to not be able to watch very much of it.) It is, simply put, excruciatingly pornographic.

This is not to say for a moment that devotional preaching is a bad thing. Devotional preaching, or "springboard preaching" in which the Bible text introduces the theme of the message, can be an effective tool in the hands of the right preacher. It gives a cross-section of the man. If the preacher is a good man, devoted, mature, balanced, knowledgeable in the Scriptures, and dedicated to pleasing God, then Christians can be blessed, edified, inspired, and taught. The down side of devotional preaching is that good men practicing devotional preaching set that method up as an example for younger aspiring preachers who themselves absolutely need a very short leash to Scripture. God spare us from the religious philosophy of a 25 year old! In fact, my advice to such a well-meaning young man would be to throw away the leash for a few years and <u>grab the Bible by the collar with both hands</u>. That is the ONLY way you are going to be a blessing to the mature, older Christians in any church.

Get yourself some of the incredibly powerful study tools available everywhere today dirt cheap. Do some word studies. Learn about the grammatical elements of the Greek text of the Bible such as tense, voice, and mood at the very least. Study the cultural and historical context of the passages you preach on. Learn some apologetics. Find out what is going on in the field of biblical archaeology and Creation Science.

Study Walter Brown's Hydroplate Theory of the Flood. Read the scientific commentaries on Genesis and Revelation written by Henry Morris. Leave the devotional preaching to those who have lived in the Bible a few decades longer than you and who have read through it a few dozen times more than you have.

The other kind of preaching is of course topical preaching. Like expository preaching, this is not a lazy man's craft. If you are willing to seriously study, topical preaching can be a great tool in exegeting "the whole counsel of God" to build up solid Christians in the church.

Jack Schaap used devotional preaching to make himself king. He envisioned himself as not only king of First Baptist Church of Hammond, but as "King of Fundamentalism." Why else would anyone so aggressively promote the concept that he was beyond criticism? This is the legal premise of "Sovereign Immunity" found in the legal system, making it impossible in some jurisdictions to sue the government. This stems back from English law when the King was thought to be a divinely appointed and representative figure. They got this concept from the Romans who deified their emperors. To sue a sovereign was then to sue God, and that could not be done. To criticize either of the two Jacks was the very same thing at First Baptist Church of Hammond. This was a culture of unvarnished hero worship, plain and simple.

Hyles and Schaap made the most of this in claiming that to criticize them was to **"lift your hand against God's anointed."** Really? When did this anointing occur? Under whose authority? Is there a certificate we can see? Did Hyles or Schaap host a lavish and spectacular coronation as did Napoleon in Notre Dame Cathedral on December 2nd, 1804? Napoleon hired the famous Neoclassical artist Jacques-Louis David to commemorate it all on a canvas measuring over 500 square feet. In fact, the Hyles mural portrait on the side of the educational building across from the old church auditorium measured FIVE TIMES the size of Napoleon's painting! (See appendix) Like Napoleon, Hyles and Schaap had a masterful understanding of the dynamics of the cult of personality and the sophisticated craft of shaping a public image. Saddam Hussein, in like fashion plastered his portrait on many buildings.

So convinced was Napoleon that there was no authority greater than his own that at the last moment, to the hushed gasps of the adoring and massive crowd in Notre Dame Cathedral, HE TOOK THE CROWN FROM THE HANDS OF POPE PIUS VII AND CROWNED HIMSELF! I think that Napoleon's name should have been the two Jack's middle names.

I remember when I lived in Paris, and one day I visited "Les Invalides," the place where Napoleon is entombed. As you walk in, you see a great marble balustrade encircling a grand, round opening to a lower level. As you approach the opening, you look down to the floor below and see Napoleon's massive, deep maroon sarcophagus on a large white marble pedestal. You feel amazingly close to history as you look down upon the vessel that contains the remains of the famous French Emperor, Napoleon Bonaparte. As I looked down upon it, my grandmother leaned over to me and began sharing with me in hushed tones one of the hundreds of history lessons I was privileged to hear from the lips of a lifelong educator and administrator in the French public school system. She said to me in French. "Napoleon himself designed Les Invalides as his final resting place. Do you know why he designed the location of his sarcophagus this way, one floor below and encircled on the floor above by this marble balustrade?" I answered that I did not. She then told me: "So no one would ever be able to look upon him without bowing his head."

I never forgot that lesson. After I left First Baptist Church of Hammond in 1989, I began to think about this phrase that I heard there thousands of times: "Never lift your hand against God's anointed." I realized eventually that the biblical reference was the time that David refused to kill King Saul when he had the chance. Then I realized what this church mantra really meant: HYLES SAW HIMSELF AS A KING! As king, nobody dared hold him accountable to the standards he required of others. Jack Schaap saw himself bathed in those same stage lights. Rule J-1 on page 26 of the Hyles-Anderson College Handbook reads: "Dating Conduct must be beyond reproach, and honoring to Christ." That rule was not for the college chancellor, Jack Schaap.

Jack Schaap saw himself as a king and never let an opportunity pass to remind everyone of the crown he wore. Hyles had said publicly that "the entire spiritual fate of America rests on these two shoulders right here." This was the mantle he passed on to his son-in-law, Jack Schaap. To say that Schaap wore it proudly is like calling Niagra Falls moisture. Like Hyles, Schaap thought that this mantle made him invulnerable. Little did he understand that like the fictional Superman, there was this thing called Kryptonite. One day someone found a piece of that Kryptonite, put it in a slingshot, and nailed Schaap right between the eyes, and down he went. Schaap's Kryptonite was just like Hyles', and Napoleon's, and Sadam's, and all the other self-anointed sycophants stealing the glory that belongs to a holy God. Their Kryptonite was the accountability that is eventually thrust upon every selfanointed king.

Napoleon and Schaap were for me two peas in a pod. Napoleon cheated on his wife Josephine his entire adult life. She died of pneumonia the day he sailed to his exile in Elba, and he did not even know it. In the end, Napoleon could still only think of himself. There lay one million dead French soldiers in his wake, and two million more throughout Europe. He had forgotten the hundreds of smoking villages and the thousands of prisoners whom he had executed in cold blood, as well as the thousands of women raped by his Grande Armée. In spite of all of this, Napoleon never expressed regret, remorse, or shame. Even in exile, he welcomed the pathologically twisted adulations of the Elban citizens who shouted as he arrived, "Eviva l'Imperati!" (Long live the emperor)

"I am the Lord: that is my name: and my glory will I not give to another,"
Isaiah 42:8

"Did the man who required others to go weekly ever go himself? Did he bear fruit? Were there any Jack Hyles converts in the Hammond mega-church? The answer to that question was a resounding and hypocritical "NO!""

Chapter

8

The King Was Pleased

If you have heard my testimony, you know that I became a Christian as a result of two ladies from a Baptist Church in San Diego knocking on my door one morning, Bibles in hand. Twelve hours before, I had prayed a prayer to God about finding a good church: "Dear God, if there is a good church out there and you show me where it is, I'll go. Amen."

I was in my garden behind my home near San Diego at ten o'clock the next morning when I heard a knock on my door. I was reading Dietrich Bonhoeffer's book, *"The Cost of Discipleship."* I put the book down and went to my front door. There was Betty Storie, (See appendix) an angel of God divinely appointed to be the answer to my prayer of the night before, however stark and mechanical my simple prayer may have been. She and her visitation partner invited me to her church. As I stood speechless in that doorway, I had no doubt that this was the answer to my prayer. It was like getting a letter from God with my name and address on the envelope.

You can hear all about this if you listen to the Unshackled Radio Program, episode A-2948. In 2007, they did a wonderful and very accurate job of acting out my life story as an old-fashioned radio drama. That production has been one of the great honors of my Christian life. It has reached three million people in thirty-seven countries and been translated into twelve languages. To God be the glory!

When I began to understand more fully what had happened to me, and what the new birth was in fact all about, I took careful stock of my new life. I began to better understand what I had just received, and also the manner in which it had all come about. God had not written in the sky. He had not sent an archangel to flutter down from the clouds and explain salvation to me. He had commissioned two very average ladies from a Baptist church in a small Southern California town. They had been faithfully taught by an obedient, dedicated and faithful pastor, Pastor Dorman Owens, to be true to the Great Commission on a weekly basis. He had been their consistent personal example. Thankfully for me, they had learned well.

Having understood these things, I very quickly established in my own mind the importance of doing the very same thing. I told Pastor Dorman that any time he was going to go out and knock on doors to present the truths that these two ladies represented at my doorstep, that I would be willing to go with him.

I was awed at the power that I felt because of the source of this commission from God and the eternal difference its presentation could make in the life of anyone willing to hear it. Soon we were going out every week, and often two or three times in a week. Pastor Dorman never, ever put any emphasis on numbers, nor has he ever to this day tallied how many people he has led to Christ. What I do know is this: he pastored for 38 years and he was continually faithful to the Great Commission, going out several times a week for several hours each time. I also know that he understood the role of repentance and discipleship in evangelism.

It is nearly impossible to have a conversation with Pastor Dorman without some flowing and natural references to the many men and women he has led to Christ who are now pastors, evangelists, missionaries, or just solid and productive Christians who have raised another generation to serve God. He came back into my home the following week after my visit to his church and we sat with an open Bible between us. He explained to me the doctrine of salvation in a thorough, patient and methodical manner. This was the farthest thing there was from the "One, two, three repeat-after-me" method of First Baptist Church of Hammond.

When I got to Hyles-Anderson College the following fall, I was already committed to evangelism in a very serious way. Their methodology was a perfect fit for me, because it was really nothing more than salesmanship, and I knew salesmanship well and was very good at it. I had made a good living in sales in San Diego in the solar energy business. I was one of those proverbial people of whom others often said, "He could sell refrigerators to Eskimos."

Every week I turned in my tally of "saved souls" as was required. I never kept track of numbers, but in the three years that I spent as an undergraduate at Hyles-Anderson College, they apparently piled up. Just before my graduation in 1986 I was told that I was going to be the recipient of "The Sword of the Lord For Evangelism." They told me that this meant that I had "won more souls" than anyone in that graduating class. I don't remember the figure they gave me, and I don't care today one whit what it was, but it was in the thousands. How many of those folks were really saved? Probably precious, precious few.

A number of years ago, I was in a discussion of those days and those methods on an Internet forum. I began to ask myself if I remembered any reference to Jack Hyles having any converts of his own. Did the man who required others to go weekly ever go himself? Did he bear fruit? Were there any Jack Hyles converts in the Hammond mega-church? I strongly suspected that the answer to that question was a resounding and hypocritical "NO!" Neither did I recall that question ever being raised in my six years there. Of course, the Hyles people on the forum said that there were "many" converts of his in the church and all over the country and that "he went soul winning regularly." I knew otherwise, so I played dumb and took great delight in at first agreeing with them that of course there surely had to be, and then asking on that forum if anyone could name one Jack Hyles convert.

There were hundreds of folks on that major forum, but patient though I was, not one person could step up and name a single Jack Hyles convert. The closest anyone could come was a young girl who had reached Hyles by dialing a wrong number in his Michigan motel room while he was on a preaching trip there. He supposedly was able to "win her to the Lord." Of course he paraded her all over the place, including before Pastor's School. Not long after that, the young woman sadly took her own life. Did she too fall victim to one of the cadre of sexual predators at First Baptist Church of Hammond? Only God knows.

One day in March, perhaps around 1988, I got a call from Eddie Lapina. My "soul winning" prowess was by then well known. Lapina also knew that I had a video camera. There were not many of those around in the 1980's. Pastor's School was right around the corner and Jack Hyles had asked Lapina if it would be possible to get an unstaged video of one of the church's "soul winners" "leading someone to Christ." Lapina asked me if I thought I could pull it off.

As luck would have it, I had just had some positive results the Saturday before with a woman in Lake Station, not far from Hammond. I had asked her then if we could come back to present the Gospel to her husband, as he was not there when we first came. She agreed. I did not want to ruin this opportunity by dragging my 1980's giant video camera into their living room, but I brought it along just in case and kept it in the car. Her husband was home and when I saw that he was open to what we had shared with his wife, I asked them both if I could set a camera up in the corner so as to later be able to teach other Christians "how to introduce Jesus Christ" to those who wanted to know Him. To my delight, they agreed.

I ran to the car, grabbed the camera and tripod and came back in the house and quickly set it all up as discreetly as possible in a corner of the living room. Soon, the Hyles brand of evangelism known as "Roman's Road" was in full swing. Of course, I was very conscious of the importance of doing a good job here. Sadly, this may have been more because of my understanding of where this video tape was going than for any purely spiritual reason. I was a king worshiper back then, like everyone I was surrounded with seven days a week. The fact that his anointing had been of his own hand mattered little to me then, if at all.

The next day I handed the tape to Eddie Lapina and told him that I had managed to do what he had asked and that I hoped it would be what "Brother Hyles" had in mind. Within a day my phone rang. It was Eddie Lapina. He said to me, "Brother Hyles saw the tape." I eagerly asked him, "Did he like it?" His immediate answer was, "He went nuts over it." I recall vividly that I was not at all sure what that meant. Did he like it or was he for some reason infuriated at some aspect of the presentation? Lapina used a string of highly complimentary superlative terms in doing his best to describe that Hyles' liking for the tape was over the top, and then some. The king was very happy, and that was a good thing for me.

Pastor's School was right around the corner, and the programs had already been printed. The Pastor's School attendance in those days was always in the 5,000 range. They packed out the church auditorium on Sibley Street. So enamored was Hyles with my video that they had the thousands of Pastor's School programs redone. Prominently featured on the new programs was a daily seminar on "soul winning" where my tape would be shown. I would be there to teach what I knew to the thousands of pastors and other Christian leaders in attendance. I am fairly sure that no Hyles-Anderson College student had ever taught at Pastor's School. I had learned their craft well, and the king was pleased.

Chapter

9

Pornography - The Unseen Force

Very often in astronomy, when a new heavenly body is discovered, there is an important astronomical principle involved. It is not unusual to see the gravitational influence on a heavenly body, yet not be able to see the object exerting that influence. Calculations are then made to determine the location and mass of the hidden object based on the influence that it is observed to have on the visible object. Often when astronomers search that area of the universe with a general idea of the hidden object's mass and distance, the hidden object is then discovered. This is what I see when I look at the life of Jack Schaap. That hidden object can, in my view, be only one thing: pornography.

The strategy of the Devil has never changed. He is out to corrupt everything that God called "good" and to offer a perverted counterfeit. Satan has never changed his method. He began with Eve in the Garden of Eden when he subtly tried to create doubt in her mind as to the words that God had spoken to her and Adam: *"Yeah, hath God said?"* I hear it this way: *"Yeah, hath God sssssssssssaid?"*

God has given the institutions of marriage and family to the human race. It is, in particular, within the institution of

71

marriage that the sexual urges that are part of our created natures are designed to be satisfied. Married Christian couples often confuse their counterparts in the unregenerate world when they express that their marriage just seems to get better and better as it matures. This is the diametric opposite of what happens when fulfillment is sought outside of the moral parameters of marriage. Genuine and lasting satisfaction is never found. It was not designed that way.

Pornography tempts many whose unbelief is acted out on its stage. I believe that Jack Schaap traveled this road for many years. I know from personal observation that he was very close with Dave Hyles when Dave was advertising for group sex in a Chicago porn magazine and punctuating those ads with naked pictures of his wife performing sex acts. Those pictures went public in Adam Magazine in September of 1989, June of 1990 and March of 1991: *"IL: Clean, discreet attractive lady looking for bi-ladies or couples to join with my husband and variety of sexual possibilities."* A total of eight of these advertisements were a part of the record of Dave Hyles' activities that emerged in the late 1980's and early 1990's. When Hyles learned of this he implored Pastor School delegates not to take the handouts illustrating these ads being distributed on the street in front of the church: *"The boy has done something awful, and I prefer that you not look at it."* The "boy" was thirty-six years old.

The reasons that I can say with confidence that Jack Schaap was involved with pornography is that first of all, he admits to watching pornography on the Internet, though he calls it inadvertent. The second reason is that there is nothing else on the face of the earth that can better explain the pornographic object lesson that has now made Schaap the laughingstock of YouTube with his "Polished Shaft" sermon. If you plan on seeing it for the first time, I must warn you: this is an excruciatingly difficult thing to watch. Lastly, it becomes evident to even the casual observer that Jack Schaap engaged in a disturbing and even pathological sexualization of such Bible teachings as the Lord's Supper and a Christian's relationship to the Bible. This material can all be found in his book, *"Marriage: The Divine Intimacy,"* (pp 42,43, & 44).

Pathetically, Schaap gets the meaning of his two key Hebrew words completely, thoroughly and utterly wrong! He interprets David's verb "laid" in Psalm 119:30, *"Thy judgments have I laid before me,"* as follows: "That word 'laid' is a sexual term which literally means the same thing as a man laying with a woman." Schaap could not be more wrong about this. "Laid" is the Hebrew word *"Shavah"* which means, "equal, like, compared or profit." It is further translated as "to agree with, to become like, to resemble, to be like, equivalent." *(Strong's Complete Dictionary of Bible Words, p530).*

Schaap goes on to also sexualize another phrase that follows in Psalm 119: *"I have stuck to thy testimonies."* In his own words from the same book: "That word 'stuck' means the act of a man entering his wife; it is sexual intercourse." He is completely wrong once again. The word "stuck" in Psalm 119 is the Hebrew word *"Dabaq."* It means to cleave, to overtake, to keep fast, to abide, or to be pursued. The preferred meaning is "to pursue closely." Schaap also is on record as calling the Lord's Supper "spiritual intercourse."

He has also taught that when a man gives into his lower nature and is overtaken by lust, it is because "one of our ancestors allowed sexual sin to come into his or her life, then an unclean spirit invades that family. The unclean spirit may be dormant for a long time just waiting for the right time to rear his ugly head." Schaap calls this "a hidden trigger ... that causes the person to cross lines. That trigger is dormant iniquity lying in the hearts of mankind placed there by previous generations. When a person doesn't deal with his ancestors' sexual sins, those sins come back and haunt that person again and again. Christians need to confess the sins of their fathers." *(Marriage: The Divine Intimacy, p 51)*

Sorry Jack! My Bible says,

> ***"Now the works of the flesh are manifest, which are these; Adultery, fornication, uncleanness, lasciviousness, They which do such things shall not inherit the kingdom of God."***
> Galatians 5:19, 21

Even in the face of this PUBLISHED doctrinal deviancy, PASTORS CONTINUED SENDING THEIR YOUNG PEOPLE TO HYLES-ANDERSON COLLEGE, AND INVITING SCHAAP TO PREACH IN THEIR CHURCHES AND TO HEADLINE THEIR MAJOR CONFERENCES! They also legitimized an abhorently corrupt man by standing in his pulpit. What shame and contempt these men deserve!

In fact, what Schaap was saying was that his lust had gotten out of his control. He could not find the handle on it any more than could his notorious brother-in-law Dave Hyles, with whom he hung around regularly. (One evening there was a knock on our door in Lake Station, Indiana and I looked out only to see them both standing side by side on our front porch. My wife was horrified.)

The fact that one man can go horribly wrong when given unlimited power, respect, authority and adulation is not new. It was Lord Acton who first authored the phrase, "Power corrupts, and absolute power corrupts absolutely." I get that. Here, however, is what I will never get: why didn't SOMEBODY on that platform stand up when Schaap was literally MASTURBATING WITH A STICK OF WOOD in his now infamous sermon, "A Polished Shaft?" Why did one of those men not have the manhood and decency to stop this incredible and truly insane display of unimaginable vulgarity? Where were you, my old skiing buddy Roy Moffit?

Where were you, my Concentrated Evangelism teacher Ray Young? Where were you my co-worker in the youth ministry, Eddie Lapina?

What about you men of the church who were in that audience that night with your young daughters? COULD YOU NOT MUSTER THE MORAL BACKBONE OR THE DECENCY AS FATHERS TO MARCH YOUR DAUGHTERS OUT OF THAT BUILDING WHERE PORNOGRAPHY WAS ON DISPLAY FROM A PULPIT? I am sorry, but that is something I will never understand if I live to be one hundred years old!

How else does the rational mind explain what is obvious to the 100,000 who have viewed this pornographic experience called a sermon? How can a man calling himself a Baptist preacher put pornography on display IN A PULPIT and not understand that he is before a Christian gathering of young people, and not on a stage in a strip club as a warm-up act to pole dancers! How does the conscience become so calloused and so fatally seared and any vestige of decency evaporate to the extent that any man would dare to pollute a pulpit in a Baptist Church with such a tawdry and unthinkable depiction of a gratuitous sex act? The answer is simple: **that mind has been so filled with pornography as to no longer be able to distinguish moral right from wrong** or Christian purity and restraint from public masturbation. This is the level to which Jack Schaap had sunk, and there was not a man in that church with the backbone or enough Christian decency to run to him and simply say: ENOUGH!

I am sorry, First Baptist Church of Hammond, but you do not deserve to be healed. **You deserve to be disbanded in disgrace!** You staff men have known of Jack Schaap's regular display of gutter vulgarity for many years. Some of you have witnessed the physical abuse he has heaped on young men in his office, and even your own friends and co-workers. I have

75

heard the accounts from those present, (see Appendix) and I don't understand to save my life why assault charges were not in some instances forthcoming. WHY DID YOU PUT UP WITH THIS from this man? Did you really think that a holy God was going to look the other way? Did you really and truly believe that blasphemous drivel peddled by Hyles about "not to go into the other person's area of judgment and criticize even if we know the facts..." *(Jack Hyles on Justice,* p 25). Did any of you ever think of trying to find support in the Bible for this twisted and deviant doctrine? Did this not begin at some point to sound like the pathological and lunatic ravings of a man-centered CULT?

Have you ever heard of the BEREANS? Have you ever read of a godly man in the Bible by the name of Samuel whom God plainly told to judge Eli the high priest *"because his sons made themselves vile and he restrained them not."* (I Samuel 3) Could there be a closer parallel to this biblical account than Jack Hyles, his son Dave Hyles, and Schaap's publicly simulated masturbation in the PULPIT? For the love of God, **WHAT IS WRONG WITH YOU FIRST BAPTIST CHURCH STAFF MEN?**

Paul exhorted Timothy to expose false teachers, and Paul named the names of Hymaneus and Philetus as an example of how to deal with false teachers (II Timothy 2:16-18). Not only did these compromised and servile staff men lack the backbone to challenge Hyles or Schaap, but THEY WOULDN'T EVEN READ THE ACCUSATIONS AND PROOF PRESENTED BY GOOD MEN ACROSS THIS LAND WHO HAD THE MANHOOD AND CHRISTIAN DECENCY TO BRING THE OBVIOUS CHARGES FORWARD!

They blindly followed the teachings of Jack Hyles who saw any and all accusations as slander and ignored a thousand times the biblical admonitions and protocols of church discipline found throughout the Scriptures. Hyles' refusal to discipline corrupt abusers of the innocent only resulted in more victims. It resulted in more ruined lives, and thousands of once well-intentioned and sincere followers of Jesus Christ who understandably today have nothing but contempt and disdain for the cause of Fundamentalism, if not the very cause of Christ. Can men like these lay any claim whatsoever to the name of Christ in their lives and so-called ministries and abide the filth and abuse of thirty years without uttering a word? For the love of a holy God, I DON'T SEE HOW! Did the "Bobbleheads" not have two brain cells to rub together or an elementary school level of Biblical understanding sufficient to challenge Hyles' teaching that "If you ever lose your heroes, you lose your security." ARE YOU KIDDING ME??? **JESUS CHRIST IS SUPPOSED TO BE YOUR HERO!**

Did not anyone have the intelligence to correct the church organist, Elaine Colsten, when she wrote in her book, *"As I See Church Music:"* "As an organist, I cannot separate the two—God and my pastor." Did not someone have the sense born of rudimentary biblical literacy to inform her: **JESUS CHRIST DIED ON THE CROSS FOR YOUR SINS, NOT JACK HYLES!**

How could those staff men decide to say nothing when one of their own with whom they shared the platform every Sunday had an affair with the wife of a college student from California in 1986, and Hyles shuffled him off to a Texas church without offering to so much as to sit down and pray with the decimated husband, or their five children? Twenty-six years later, these children have still not seen their father. There were too many of these men that Hyles relocated in the identical manner that the Catholic Church reassigned pedophile priests hundreds of times. I pray that you did not add to your sin of indulging adulterers with your complicit silence by displaying an unspeakably hypocritical condemnation of these Catholic clerics. But you know what? I'm willing to bet that you did!

How could you ignore the veritable MOUNTAIN of evidence:

- *Fundamental Seduction*: the Jack Hyles Case, by V.A. Glover; 485 pages
- *The Wizard of God, My Life With Jack Hyles*, by Vic Nischick, former deacon and husband of Hyles' mistress, Jennie Nischick.
- *The Saddest Story We Ever Published*, by Robert Sumner in the Biblical Evangelist in1989 featuring many first-hand accounts of Hyles' chronic sins.
- *An Open Letter to Jack Hyles* by my dear friend of thirty years Hyles-Anderson professor George Godfrey, imploring Hyles to remove the door between his office and his secretary Jennie Nischick's office.
- *Sin in the Camp of Fundamentalism*, a report by a large group of Independent Baptist pastors who saw Hyles' abuses for what they truly were.
- *Preying from the Pulpit,* a full length documentary of First Baptist Church of Hammond. I was privileged to have a part in this as it bore witness to the cultic nature of your church under Jack Hyles.
- Linda Hyles Murphrey's twelve minute Ted Video detailing her growing up in the Hyles home. [http://www.youtube.com/watch?v=eJsOlLqBEyo]
- The many Internet Forums in which the victims of the abuse have been speaking out in detail for many years.

I was an integral part of your "Big Days" and saw you cook the numbers over and over again. I was instructed on several of these occasions to go into the projects and fill the buses with little black boys and girls whom we were otherwise explicitly told by Ray Young to never bring into the church auditorium. We preached to them on the buses and drove them down the alley behind the church so you could then count their "professions of faith" since "they were made on church property," to quote Jack Hyles.

Eddie Lapina, I was in your office at the bus kids' high school in 1986 when you scolded a black teenage boy named Jeff because he had dated a Puerto Rican girl named Ivette, telling him plainly that he could not date her "because she is white."

I learned well your "One, Two Three, Repeat After me" style of "witnessing." I was a young Christian then, but I knew that there was something these kids did not have that, by the grace of God, had found its way into my heart. Hyles taught us that "repentance is changing your mind. If a man is condemned by unbelief, then if he changes his mind and believes, he has repented and is saved." I cannot count the times I heard Hyles say that. Yes, I swallowed it.

Thank God after I graduated from Hyles-Anderson College in 1986 and Hyles-Anderson seminary in 1988, I came to realize that I needed a real Christian education to separate the cultic doctrine I had learned from the occasional admixture of biblical truth that by some miracle had seeped in. That is when I went off to another seminary and earned a real Bible degree: a Ph.D. in Philosophy in Religion. After that, I used to say that when I visited a church, if I put my Hyles-Anderson diplomas in the window, I got to park in the "theologically handicapped zone." Humor always has to be based on truth to be funny, and this humorous expression was not lacking for a solid footing.

You church people heard Jack Hyles talking about praying to his dead mother, and you said nothing. You heard him clearly espouse the Catholic doctrine of praying for the dead. That was when in a sermon on February 7, 1988 entitled "Full Reward" we all heard him say that he believed that his efforts on Christ's behalf would give God a reason to be easier on his father Athie Hyles, whom he believed was in hell. (Hyles' father was never an alcohlic as Hyles said. The Hyles family in Italy, Texas says Jack Hyles' mother left him because of his adultery.)

You staff men were within feet of Jack Schaap thousands of times when he stood in the pulpit, desperate to raise money for that monument to himself, the new auditorium. There you all sat to hear him preach in the strained screams and rants that may as well have been made into a neon sign high above the church that read: IF YOU SAY IT LOUD ENOUGH, IT MUST BE SO! Like a river, the shallower Schaap got, the more noise he made, but that never occurred to you. You heard him talk jokingly about prostituting his wife to raise money for the new auditorium. That was when he announced that if he thought it would help, he would **"send my wife up to the South Side of Chicago in a miniskirt and a fur coat in the back seat of a Cadillac"** to raise the money. How utterly tasteless is this, even behind the thinly veiled pretest of humor.

How does one accord one atom of respect to any man who would sit under that kind of profane and vulgar blasphemy and heresy for decades and say NOTHING while the victim count mounted by the week? As Hyles himself was fond of screaming from his pulpit:

**"I'VE GOT MORE RESPECT FOR A PIMP
THAN MEN LIKE YOU!"**

Chapter

10

Is First Baptist Church of Hammond A Cult?

A very interesting thing happened to me after I left First Baptist Church of Hammond in 1989. I had graduated the year before from Hyles-Anderson Seminary with an M.Th., a master's degree in Pastoral Theology. This had been a two year post-graduate program into which I entered after my graduation from Hyles-Anderson College in 1986 with a B.S. in Pastoral Theology. One of the courses I took in the graduate program was a class on cults. After I parted ways with the church and became a *persona-non-grata* at my alma mater, I opened my notebook from that course one day and began to look at what they had taught as the defining characteristics of a cult. EVERY ONE OF THEM APPLIED TO FIRST BAPTIST CHURCH OF HAMMOND!

A couple of years ago I thought I would talk about those things and so I went into a studio and made a five part video series entitled, "How Does a Good Church Become a Cult." Those videos are on YouTube and have garnered many thousands of hits and hopefully helped a lot of people. I would strongly recommend that anyone reading this book watch these short videos. They average about five minutes each. Just go to YouTube and type in my name and the word "cult" and they will all come up.

One thing that you will see coming across in this video series is that, in the Christian life, the concept of liberty is a very prominent theme. The very basis of Christian salvation is being set free from the power, influence and consequence of sin.

"Where the Spirit of the Lord is, there is LIBERTY."
2 Corinthians 3:17

There is perhaps no greater indicator of ecclesiastical health than liberty. How much influence does the church have in your personal life? How far does the authority of the pulpit extend into the congregation? Is there in your church an expressed understanding of the "horizontal" aspect of church life inherent in its foundational purposes? (See Chapter 7)

The Bible teaches us, as I have discussed at length in chapter seven, that the authority of the pastor in a New Testament church is not absolute. The command in Hebrews 13:17, as we have shown, is to have the kind of man in that office in whom the church member can have FAITH! We heard over, and over, and over when I was at First Baptist Church of Hammond the phrase "Blind Loyalty." This should have been like a piercing fire siren going off in an enclosed room. Nobody seemed to be thinking in terms of what this concept meant or implied. Sadly, I have to number myself among that indiscriminate and deluded assembly for over six years.

The Bible teaches DISCERNMENT. Just read the book of Proverbs. This book of the Bible is a treatise on discernment and sound judgment. Over and over again Solomon tells his sons to exercise sound judgment regardless of the circumstances. What Jack Hyles and Jack Schaap did was to tell us that they were entitled to executive privilege, and that required you to check your discernment, your biblical standards of righteousness and your common sense at the church-house door. Sadly, we bought into this unspoken requirement without understanding that they both had an ulterior motive: THEY CRAVED POWER! Jack Hyles himself has said over and over too many times to count, that the prayer he prayed the most was "God give me power." Nobody questioned what he meant by this, but as so many former members look back on this now, we have trouble believing why we never thought to question this seemingly insatiable desire of his for power, authority and control.

The problem over the years has become a predictable one: no amount of power satisfies until it is absolute. With the diminishing of accountability that autocracy brings, the human nature at our core sheds any and all form of personal and moral restraint. You don't need to go one millimeter further than this premise to understand men like Jack Hyles and Jack Schaap.

The "meek and quiet spirit" held up to us in the descriptive example and life of Jesus Christ becomes the first casualty in a church run by men like Hyles and Schaap. The willingness to face an accusation in the same spirit as did the disciples when Jesus told them that one of them would betray Him and ask, **"IS IT I?"** (Mat. 26:25), will be non-existent in a cult church such as First Baptist Church of Hammond. Schaap had many, many warnings delivered to him by well intentioned Christians who knew that judgment would come and that it would be a devastating experience with massive collateral damage. Schaap followed Hyles' example and never so much as acknowledged any of those letters. (See the appendix for mine.)

As in many authoritarian churches, there is no mechanism for course correction, let alone dealing with the slightest criticism. The biblical phrase, **"Is it I?"** will never echo off the walls of most offices where an Independent Fundamental Baptist Pastor sits behind a desk. Yes, there are of course exceptions, and I would never discourage anyone from holding out the hope of finding one. I believe that I have beaten the odds and done that. For the first time in twenty-three years, my wife and I are in a healthy and balanced church under good leadership.

The Doctrine of the Total Depravity of Man will never be taught in the overwhelmingly vast majority of Independent, Fundamental Baptist Churches. In fact, I am undoubtedly guilty of a serious understatement here. I don't think I have ever heard this doctrine taught in my three decades as a Christian. If your church has taught this doctrine in a meaningful, systematic and thorough way, I say to you: "Congratulations!" You may well be in a healthy and balanced church. Count your blessings!

Even the good churches seem to be married to the status quo. This is the liability however of Conservatism. We are the last ones to take up the new tools. We have difficulty in drawing the line between style and core Bible doctrine. Sometimes, separation becomes isolation, and we lose a great deal of effectiveness in our ministries as a result. Too many good pastors keep an Amish hat in their closet, and when a new idea comes up, they run to put it on.

Does it really make sense to look back to the preceding era and look at the objections that were thundered from church pulpits across the land about how the piano did not belong in our worship services because it was played in honky-tonks? This is an Amish perspective, if you ask me. Pianos were no more evil than organs, and I respectfully would say to our Amish friends, the internal combustion engine and electricity are not offensive to God. I wonder if some day some Fundamentalist whackjob somewhere will proudly announce a new level of separation by refusing to drive on any highway that features billboards for whiskey or strip clubs? Lets face it and admit what we have all known for years about this crowd: theirs is just a prideful way of saying, "I HAVE

OUT-FUNDAMENTALED AND OUT-SEPARATED YOU, BROTHER!"

For many of these folks, the whole KJV issue was not about manuscript evidence but about being able to brag about being religiously superior to others—more separated, more discerning, less tolerant, more "Fundamental," and more pure. This was Jack Hyles in a nutshell, and he set that as a standard for a generation of preachers as their stamp of God's approval and superiority over others. The message was clear: I AM BETTER THAN YOU!"

The question I would ask is this: is there a mechanism or a protocol in place in your church to evaluate a change for the better in method, style or the tools of ministry? Do you think in this electronic age of instantaneous worldwide mass communication that the point of the spear of church evangelism ought to still be handing out a Roman's Road tract on the street as we did fifty years ago? Don't get me wrong, I am not suggesting by any means that this is a bad thing. What I am saying is that with a proper understanding of the new tools now available in the world that can put any church, any message, any book or any cause on an indescribably broad stage overnight, why is the church so often stuck right where we were in the 1950's? Caution toward what is new is good; sometimes fear is not.

Most anything said from a Sunday School podium lives for but a moment. Carefully crafted words and phrases incorporated into a blog post live forever, and if done well, multiply exponentially.

I am by no means an expert in this, but I can tell you without the slightest exaggeration that in the year that followed my company's communications and marketing epiphany, Omega Chemical Corporation experienced 1,000%+ growth. I can also tell you that each month there are as many as 10,000 hits on my ministry website, JERRYKBOOKS.COM, and that my testimony and other clear messages of salvation by grace through faith on that site are placed squarely before the eyes of perhaps 100,000 people each year. I am just one person, not a church congregation. Many thousands of these visitors to my websites and blogs spend an extended amount of time visiting my websites, and I think it is fair to assume that many listen to the dramatic radio production of my life story on Unshackled, as the link is very prominent on my home page. What is your church doing? Most churches have "catalogue websites" that have never reached out and grabbed one living soul. That is like putting up a website in a desert. You HAVE to drive traffic!

God expects us to be "wise as serpents," and I believe that this means using wisely and effectively the many new tools available in the great cause of Jesus Christ. Sometimes to save a drowning man, you have to jump into dirty water. That is where these people live, and that is where our Lord Jesus went to find them. If we will remember, it was the Pharisses who found fault with Him for that.

But, enough of the new tools for now. In the end, we need to understand what brought Jack Schaap down. Pastors, keep your eye on Jesus Christ! <u>THE SUREST SIGN TO ME OF A MAN IN THE PULPIT WHO HAS NOT HAD A GENUINE CLOSENESS WITH THE SAVIOR IS A LACK OF HUMILITY</u>. Don't be that man. Make sure that when you stand in the pulpit, your people will know that in the preceding week, like the Apostle John on Patmos in the presence of the Glorified Christ, you "FELL ON YOUR FACE AS DEAD."

When a Christian gets a real and powerful vision of God, he never wants to get in a pulpit and scream about it and tell others how miserable and weak they are. Rather, he comes to a view of himself such as was expressed by Daniel after he had his vision of a holy God:

"Therefore I was left alone, and saw this great vision, and there remained no strength in me: for my comeliness was turned in me into corruption, and I retained no strength."
Daniel 10:8

Where did Jack Hyles and Jack Schaap go wrong? <u>THAT</u> is where they went wrong! Their appeal was fueled by a raging, narcissistic and unchecked tidal wave of pride. Let us all learn from their mistakes. God will not share His glory with another! Once we get any kind of genuine glimpse of Jesus Christ, we will understand that surely the Psalmist's description of himself was right on the money: **"I AM A WORM."** Until you see that worm in the mirror, you have not seen Christ.

"For the time is come that judgment must begin at the house of God."
I Peter 4:17

"That suspicion was that some of these H.A.C. college students at the ongoing vigil believed that Jack Hyles would not remain in the grave."

Chapter

11

We Are More Than Conquerors

When I came to the understanding of who Jesus Christ is, it seems like it all came at once. Maybe this was because I was in an intense and serious seeking mode when I came to Christ as an adult. If you have read my testimony, Racing Toward God, or heard the dramatic radio production of my life story on the Unshackled Radio Program, you know what I am talking about.

With my salvation came a sense of empowerment and the understanding that my life now had a great and noble meaning. By empowerment, I do not mean at all anything relating just to myself, but rather having to do with whom I now represented. In particular, I attached great personal meaning to I John 4:4

> *"Greater is he that is in you,*
> *than he that is in the world."*
> 1 John 4:4

I felt an elevation of purpose compared to what my life had been up to my salvation. I also felt that I was on the winning team, and that this equipped me to deal with any challenge to righteousness anywhere. I became convinced of the authority of the Judaeo-Christian Scriptures, and understood that all religions are first and foremost defined by their scriptures, not by their adherents.

With time, I learned the importance of picking my battles. One battle that came to me with a vengeance was the hypocrisy that I began to see in the leadership of the First Baptist Church of Hammond. Few things trouble me like being set up as the victim of deception, and if hypocrisy is anything, it is brazen deception, no matter where it is found.

I remember one Sunday evening when Jack Hyles stepped into the pulpit and began tapping his shoulders with his finger tips. He did this for maybe thirty seconds without saying a word. Then he spoke: "Right here. Right here, folks. The spiritual fate of America rests on these two shoulders right here." That was the first time that anything this man said from that pulpit did not go down well for me. It was like a chicken bone that had lodged in my throat.

Not long before that incident, something else happened that gave me great pause. It happened in Hyles "Saturday Night Classes" where Hyles basically presented and taught the material from whatever book he had in the works at that time. It was geared for the "Preacher Boys," the preachers in training from Hyles-Anderson College. It was at one of those classes that Hyles stepped into the pulpit and the first words he spoke were, "Be ethical." He continued on: "Be ethical, fellas. I have just learned that someone has taken their notes from these classes and published them without my permission. That's called plagiarism, and it's wrong! Be ethical. If you're not ethical, you're nothing, and you'll never do anything for God."

I felt like I had just been hit by a truck. That person who had published those notes was me, and everyone in that auditorium knew it. It was the mid 1980's and I had the only computer in the whole college. I had taken very detailed notes in these special classes that were held every other Saturday evening at the church. When more and more students asked me for copies of my notes, I typed them out in an extensive outline, indexed it, bound it in a plastic binder and offered them to others. I knew better than to charge into this undertaking without running it by Jack Hyles, and so I did just that. He responded in a letter giving me full permission to "do with those notes whatever you see fit."

I felt like I was under a spotlight the entire time that the class went on that evening after Hyles had dropped the bomb on me. After the class I went to Hyles' office and knocked on his door. He opened the door and extended a warm greeting to me. I was high on his list, a fact that he had not failed to note in several letters he had written me during my time there. [See Appendix]. I got right to the point: "Brother Hyles, I'm the one who published those notes." He gave me a curious look and said with great surprise: "It was YOU, Jerry?" I replied, "Yes, it was me. You wrote me a letter giving me your permission to do so."

"Do you still have that letter?" Hyles asked me with an ever so slightly suspicious look on his face. That was a silly question. I suspect that most letters that anyone would receive from him were like letters received from the President: they would be framed and hung on the wall. This was even more true when the recipient of such a letter was a college student. "Yes, I do have it." He then said, "Bring it to me." That letter was under his door before eight o'clock the next morning.

Those classes being held every other Saturday evening, it was a tortuously long wait for the next one. During that time, I walked the halls of the college while attending classes and went to church three times a week feeling like I had a sign on my back saying, "I am the unethical plagiarist who will never amount to anything that Dr. Hyles talked about."

I was practically counting the hours until the next Saturday Night Class. There was not a shred of doubt in my mind that Hyles would then fully exonerate me publicly. What else could "God's man" possibly do for the person he had often called "my buddy?" After all, my character and reputation, the stock in trade of every Preacher Boy, had sustained massive damage. I was in a very tough situation because of that. I felt that if I shared the true facts with anyone, I was making Hyles look bad. That was a death sentence in that institution. I had gained much favor there in general and with Hyles in particular, and I knew better than to give even the slightest appearance that I was challenging the man, even though I knew full well that I had done nothing wrong and that he had acted badly at great personal expense to me.

Finally the time came and Hyles stepped into the pulpit to teach the next Saturday Night Class. I thought that this was certainly going to be the venue for the apology. In fact, I thought that there was a very good chance that he would even try to make up for his gaffe by heaping some personal praise upon me, or at the very least by referring to me from the pulpit affectionately the way he had in several personal letters he had written to me.

The class started with an impromptu, goofball skit by a self-appointed delegation of preacher boys, as was the tradition before those classes. Then the lesson started. No mention of the incident from the previous class was made. I then reasoned to myself that he would do it at the end of the class. It was inconceivable to me that he would neglect to make things right before the same crowd that he had so badly diminished me. The class ended. He folded up his notes and walked out the door a few steps up from the pulpit in the tenor section of the choir. He had spoken not a word about me, the notes, or the letter.

I was devastated. That was when I first came face to face with a realization that was beyond unthinkable for me: Jack Hyles had a major flaw in his character! In fact, it was undoubtedly unthinkable as well for any of the 5,000 churchmembers who filled the auditorium each week at 523 Sibley Street in Hammond. We all came to hear the man we had all collectively anointed as "the greatest preacher of our time." Take that level of adulation and multiply it by ten, and you have the sentiment of each and every one of the 2,300 students at Hyles-Anderson College toward Jack Hyles.

This was the closest that I ever came to being personally abused in my seven years in the church and college. My saving grace was probably that I had a reputation that was able to survive such a devastating assault on my character. Still, it was not a good time to be me. The passing of time seemed to smooth over the wounds, but the scar remained prominent, at least to me. Fortunately, I came from a strong and stable family, who though not Christians, did not ever foster a need in me to make any institution my substitute parents.

After Hyles died, I drove past memory Lane on US 30 in Crown Point, Indiana. I don't know if it was formally organized, but college students were there at all hours of the day and night in front of the man's crypt 24/7 for many weeks after his death. I do not want to be accused of overstating this, but there was a suspicion that came to my mind and would not go away. Let me be clear that this is all it was—a suspicion. <u>That suspicion was that some of these college students believed that Jack Hyles would not remain in the grave.</u> The fact that others who saw what I saw also had this nagging suspicion testifies to the status that this man had in the eyes of Hyles-Anderson College students in 2001.

This man for whom I would have gone to the ends of the earth had just shown me that the personal friendship he had declared for me and the appreciation that he had often expressed for all that I had accomplished for him could never rise to the level of prompting an admission of personal error on his part, even though no one would have begrudged him an oversight such as he had made. Along with the incident in his office over the business deal with the church member, I had learned my lesson, and I had learned it well: don't slip on the deck and fall off this ship, for the captain will not alter his course to come and fish you out. He will plow you over and not even feel the tiny thud you will make as you are mangled by the ship's giant propellers.

Perhaps this is similar to your experiences at First Baptist Church of Hammond, or some other cult-like church. Perhaps you also came to realize that if caring for you and understanding your deepest needs as a human being meant that the slightest unflattering light would be cast upon the church's image, you too were heading for a collision course with the ship's rumbling propellers. If you were lucky and missed them only to be left bobbing in the cold waters of an ominous and dark sea, you understood one thing for sure: those life rings and lifeboats on that great ship of state were just there for show. Oh yes, they were meticulously maintained and brightly painted, and their highly polished brass glimmered in the sun, but they would never be launched to rescue anyone who went overboard. Never!

A few years ago, my wife and I began to counsel a young woman who had left First Baptist Church of Hammond. I have to be very careful in how I tell her story. She had been devastated by her fall from the great ship of state and her own mauling by the ship's giant propellers. In fact, the ship deliberately plowed her under, and then even circled back to do it again, and again. She was so traumatized by her experience there that when I even hinted at the suggestion that she should go public with her story, she told me if I ever said anything to anyone about it, she would deny everything. So devastated was this woman that her road to recovery will be lifelong. Given the healing power of Jesus Christ, it need not be that way, of course, and I made it a point to tell her so. Jesus did not put people on a long tortuous and prolonged path of healing. He commanded them to *"take up your bed and walk!"*

I will call her Carrie (not her real name). She was a very pretty young woman who caught the eye of Jack Schaap. He soon put her into select positions within the ministries of the church/school empire that would bring her into regular and close proximity with him. To hear her tell the story, Schaap "fell in love" with her, and would later confess to her that he could not bear to lose her. She told me that this relationship that she characterized as "an inappropriate relationship" became well known in the church and that Schaap even told his wife Cindy about it, telling her that she would just have to adjust. The technique of manipulation may well have been the one that he learned from Cindy's father: "Don't cripple a ministry that is the tip of God's phalanx in the battle to save America by putting your personal needs ahead of the salvation of millions of souls." Sadly, the pathologically skewed biblical foundation of every member of First Baptist Church of Hammond gave them no basis to ever challenge that tragic misrepresentation of a holy God. That is something that continues today throughout the church, extending all the way to Mrs. Beverly Hyles, the former wife of the late Jack Hyles, and once the First Lady of First Baptist Church of Hammond.

This young woman in my story somehow gained access through her position to a number of financial records that brought her to understand that Schaap was benefitting in an inappropriate way from his position in the church. She was aware that there were those coming to the leadership of the church and telling of being abused as young children when they were in the church schools. She knew their names, and the names of their abusers. At least one of those names has not come out to this day. One had been a teacher whom my wife and I had held in high regard. She saw that the abusers were among the most recognizable names and respected individuals in the church. As she gained the confidence of a number of the staff wives, these women shared with her many stories of affairs by their husbands. She "wrote Schaap a letter exposing the truth, and he ignored it," leaving her to "work through the confusion and shame." These are Carrie's own words to me. Schaap then excoriated her publicly, although stopped short of giving her name. His rant against women on ABC's 20/20 was directed at her, she says, because she had suggested ministering to the many staff wives whose husbands had adulterous affairs. The figure that Carrie personally expressed to me was that 90% of these staff men had been unfaithful to their wives.

I have saved all of the e-mails. Here are the exact words I said to her: "Carrie, my heart goes out to you more than I can express! You don't have to become whole, you ARE whole! Your need is only to realize that through the cleansing power of Christ. I am not saying that all you have to do is click a switch. I have no doubt that the Lord has connected you with me and also my wife Gwen to help you see this all more clearly."

"Yes, I do know Schaap well, and the principal thing that stands out is that he is a clone of the old man. Cindy married the man in whom she most saw her father. Confusion and shame cannot withstand the brilliance and cleansing nature of the light of Christ. I can't even begin to tell you how completely I believe that and with what fervor. The great news is that Gwen and I have plenty of it to share, although I would much rather help you connect directly with the Source. We live on a 13 acre wildlife preserve on a private lake, and if you and your husband & children would like to come out, we have many extra rooms. (Here is a link to our place: http://jerrykbooks.com/house.htm) You are 100% welcome at any time. We would love to meet you. Carrie, don't let their slime stick to you another day! They are not worth it, and whatever they have made you to feel, it is a complete lie compared to the grace, beauty and virtue that Jesus Christ has put in you!"

Carrie responded:

"Thank you for allowing me to share my voice. I appreciate you and your wife's graciousness. What life giving words of hope!"

JK: "Gotta give Jesus all the credit, Carrie. There are no words of hope that do not have their source in Him."

"We have been dealing with victims of these heinous impostors for 25 years, starting with the little girl who was molested by A.V. Ballenger, and the 11 year old kidnap & rape victim and her family (it cost her mother her life)."

"Vic Nischik & Voyle Glover are two of my dearest friends, as is George Godfrey. There isn't much I don't know. What I do know is that God is keeping score in great detail, and in the end, evil pays the price. In the meantime, we are far from powerless. Much of this power is available to you as you deem proper and timely. We are here to support you Carrie, and to help you, to pray for you and with you, and yes, to even the score in the name of justice and righteousness far more than you ever thought possible as God would lead. That is a well worn path for me."

"Of course this needs to be under your control and expressed in a way in which you are comfortable. There is no hurry at all. I just want you to know that you have genuine power in this and that their bravado is pure fakery. They cannot withstand the truth when delivered in God's spirit."

You see, my advice to Carrie was that she had been crushed in large measure because Schaap had identified her as not having the strength and fortitude to fight back effectively, as cults and all predators do with all their victims. All abusers are bullies who want nothing to do with a fair fight. That is why there are people whom they leave alone. They know that these people will not play the role of victim. They will come out swinging and will inflict damage and draw blood. They will pull the curtain back and reveal that the "Wizard" is a pathetic and evil manipulator. Could Vic Nischick have chosen a better title for his book exposing the adultery of Jack Hyles with Jennie Nischick than *"The Wizard of God?"* You be the judge.

I have been ever so blessed in that I have, through God's grace, completely internalized my acceptance by Jesus Christ. I am "accepted in the beloved," AND SO ARE YOU! Jesus Christ and I are a majority, AND SO ARE YOU AND JESUS! I have major value to God that cannot be diminished by any human endeavor or scheme, AND SO DO YOU! You may look in the mirror and see scars, but NEVER LET ANY SCAR OR WOUND DEFINE WHO YOU ARE. THE BEAUTY OF CHRIST THAT DWELLS IN YOU IS WHO YOU ARE! Jesus has scars He did not deserve, too. He loved you enough to undergo the tortuous death of the cross for you, and every drop of red and darkened blood that dripped on Calvary's mount was an expression of what you personally mean to Him. How can even the devil himself ever diminish that?

Every believer is a NEW CREATURE IN CHRIST! That does not, dear friend, refer to a one-time event of metamorphosis. This is the daily renewal that comes through growing as a Christian. You were elevated by God to be MORE THAN A CONQUEROR! Could there be a word in the English language that is more antithetical to the word "victim" than the word CONQUEROR?

Now I would like to dissect the methodology of Jack Hyles, Jack Schaap, and all cult leaders. I have always thought that a good window into how this dynamic operates is the guilty husband scenario. If an innocent man is suspected of infidelity by his wife, he will have a very predictable reaction: *"Honey, I don't know where you heard this, but I want you to get that person over here IMMEDIATELY. I want them to come with any and all evidence they have, and to bring anyone along whom they claim is a witness to these accusations. If they won't come, then we are getting in the car this minute and driving to their house and knocking on their front door until they open it."* THE INNOCENT MAN WANTS TO TURN UP THE LIGHT AS BRIGHT AS IT WILL GO!

The guilty man, however, does not operate according to this method. For the guilty man, light is not a friend. A guilty man in this same scenario will paint himself as the victim and use guilt to manipulate the accusing spouse. His conversation with her will go something like this: *"Sweetheart, what are you saying? Is that all that my love means to you, that you would believe vicious lies and rumors from hateful people? Honey, I thought that our relationship was on a higher plane than that. I thought you knew how much I love you. How can you doubt that I love you like this? This is crushing to me, coming from you. How could you hurt me so with these kinds of suspicions?"* (Insert theatrics and melodrama here.)

If you can cry on cue as Jack Hyles taught his preacher boys to do, you will win this round convincingly. Your strategy is to have your wife feel sorry for you and to create guilt and then leverage her guilt to your advantage. Women cannot bear the thought of being hurtful to others. As a first-line strategy in the face of the suspicion of infidelity, this method has a very high success rate.

Now if one injects into this tried and true formula for manipulating a victim of abuse the hardened steel handcuffs in the pocket of every loyal supporter of First Baptist Church of Hammond, you will have predictably and consistently neutralized any opposition. I am speaking of the fabricated doctrine found nowhere in the New Testament of **"Raising Your hand Against God's Anointed."** What a bill of goods this ruse has been the last fifty years! It is as if the requirement for entrance into the sanctuary is to check your critical thinking at the door. Along with it, we were expected to remove from our pockets our personal responsibility to maintain righteousness and leave it at the church door. It was almost as if there was a "discernment detector" at every church door, and people wanted to get the discernment out of their pockets for fear that it would set the alarm off.

We failed to be on guard for anything in the church that would overturn it, never considering that any institution run by and comprised of mortal and sinful human beings was going to be prone to imperfection. In fact, upon second glance, we can now realize that men like Jack Hyles, Dave Hyles and Jack Schaap claimed something akin to executive privilege in areas of basic Christian conduct. I have called this the "Samson Syndrome." It essentially postulates that a person can become so indispensable to God that the spiritual and moral laws which apply to everyone else do not, in their view, apply to them. I think that it is safe to say that this tendency goes even farther than this in its audacious and blasphemous premise: we are told that to be critical of such a leader is to lift one's hand against God! This reinforces one thing above everything else to me: blasphemy, like all sins, does not have a level surface with solid footing; it is a crumbling, steep and treacherous slope. Pride, in other words, is not a static condition. It is like using heroin: the amount needed to satisfy will never stop increasing, eventually resulting in a fatal overdose. This is what happened to Jack Schaap.

If you were a part of that church and were deprived of the necessary spiritual food to make possible those debilitating payments on those daily deliveries of that pride, there is complete healing available to you. **You are a child of the**

100

King, and the King does not willingly let His children suffer! He does not want them to be fodder to feed the beast of anyone's self-exaltation. He is a loving Father standing at your bedroom door. He hears the trembling sobs coming from within, and while respecting your personal privacy, He gently knocks. He has a hug for you, and His hugs always make things better. . . WAY BETTER!

If you have been victimized by First Baptist Church of Hammond or any other cult-like church that operates according to the cult model of church polity, then there are two books that are a MUST READ for you:

Toxic Faith
The Subtle Power of Spiritual Abuse

The unfortunate reality in dealing with these groups is, that YOU CANNOT WIN THE BATTLE & STAY IN THE GROUP. You have to leave! Sadly, these cult churches have learned how to make people ever so dependent on them. Sometimes that can make leaving excruciatingly difficult. If you are on staff in a cult church, your leaving will often cost you dearly: job, house, career, prestige, reputation, affection, power, automobiles, your children's education, sometimes your spouse and more. This raises the bar of freedom, independence and self-respect to a level that few will be willing to leap. They will often be disowned by even their own families. That is when the reality of who Jesus Christ is may be the only asset you have. Thank God, it is also the only asset you need.

At times like these, a believer has to BURY THEMSELVES IN SCRIPTURE. I would highly recommend Psalms. There is a principle that I believe in that occurred to me once upon relating Bible reading to my many years of SCUBA diving. I am a Certified Master Diver and have been diving in oceans on three continents. The principle is this: THE DEEPER

YOU GO, THE WETTER YOU GET. How can a person get any wetter than when they are fully submersed in water, you may ask. Well, the answer, though perhaps in a way a theoretical one, is this: the deeper you go, the greater the pressure. On the surface, the water is exerting a pressure on you of about 15 lbs. per square inch. At a depth of 132 feet, that pressure has increased to about 60 lbs. per square inch. In a way, that makes you wetter, because the water is pressing much harder on your body. I once dove to a depth of 270 feet off Diamond Rock in Martinique in the French West Indies. The water pressure there was over 120 lbs. per square inch. The way I look at it, I was "wetter" than the guy splashing around at the surface. This is the principle that I would apply to one's relationship with the Word of God in times of crisis, and beyond. GO DEEP, and STAY LONG!

There was, a number of years ago, a very trying time for me. I thank the Lord that I followed this course. Between prayer and the Word of God, I slowly emerged from a very difficult and arduous episode in my life. For a while, though, I could do little but pray and read Psalms. After thirty minutes of this, I would maybe function in my office for five or ten minutes before being overwhelmed with depression. After a while, the ratios began to change: an hour with God gave me the spiritual momentum to work a little longer than just a few minutes. After a few weeks, I was enjoying a normal schedule and I could function productively.

I remember a "conversation" with the Lord from those days that came in the midst of one of those long prayer sessions. It went something like this:

Jesus: "You are troubled, aren't you, Jerry."
Me: "Yes, I sure am Lord."
Jesus: "Well, I guess I don't blame you."
Me: "Really?"
Jesus: "Oh yes. I mean . . . . after all . . . . I have really let

102

you down in the past, haven't I?"

Me: "Uh . . . well . . . uh . . . I . . .n . . . . "

Jesus: "I guess after all these times of not being there for you when you needed Me, there is no reason for you to expect that I'll come through for you now . . . is there, Jerry . . . . ?"

Me: "Well . . . . . uh . . . . . I . . . . . uh . . . . . "

And that was how the Lord literally shamed me out of my self pity. It was one of those times when I stood up straight and tall . . . and walked out under a closed door.

"And who is he that will harm you, if ye be followers of that which is good? But and if ye suffer for righteousness' sake, happy are ye: and be not afraid of their terror, neither be troubled;"
I Peter 3:13-14

"I will never leave thee, nor forsake thee."
Heb:13:5

*"The 'meek and quiet' spirit of the
Lord Jesus went by the wayside,
if in fact it ever existed at all in
that pulpit."*

Chapter

12

Is Jack Schaap A Saved Man?

This question as it related to Jack Hyles came up over and over again in the Jack Hyles days. I had only been a Christian for a few years back then, and in all honesty, I was probably not suitably equipped to deal with that issue in a biblically meaningful and exhaustive manner. My scriptural vantage point provided me with a general understanding of the direction in which the truth would be found, but like the blind man after the first touch of Christ, *"I saw men as trees."* For reasons that will be brought out here as they apply to the salvation of Jack Schaap, I see this issue much more clearly now and supported by a broader and deeper biblical foundation.

First of all, the person who would confess and affirm the basic requirements to be a Christian, and even add to that a belief in the basic biblical doctrines of Christianity should be given some initial credibility in terms of their position in the faith. However, as I have pointed out in an exegesis of Hebrews 13:17 in chapter seven, the word for faith used throughout the New Testament does not refer at all to a mere mental assent. It translates literally as "to roll upon," indicating an existential if not a dynamic COMMITMENT

105

to that doctrine by action and lifestyle, based on complete trust and confidence. This is the utter antithesis of the "1-2-3-Repeat-After-Me" approach to evangelism that has been the hallmark of First Baptist Church of Hammond for a half a century. As one's focus on this deeper understanding develops over time, we must see in the tradition of John the Baptist that this has mandatory implications as to how we both view and present ourselves following the new birth. John said of Jesus, *"I must decrease and he must increase."* This is the key for us here in dealing with the issue of Jack Schaap's salvation, and the ability for us to understand the failure of Jack Schaap to evidence a legitimate conversion experience as a requirement of the new birth: *"...by their fruits ye shall know them."* (Mt. 7:20) What were Jack Schaap's "fruits?" That could almost have been the title of this book.

The "fruits" of Jack Schaap was the elephant in the room at First Baptist Church of Hammond. Nobody in that pulpit had shown the propensity to personally decrease or to diminish their expression of self-importance, bravado, or boastings for over five decades. It was I.F.B. swagger at its best and on a national stage. Schaap just kept that pedal to the metal and heaped upon it what eventually came to be a truckload of plain old lust. Meanwhile the bobbleheads on the platform just kept on bobbling in assent to whatever came out of the man's mouth. The meek and quiet spirit of our Savior, the Lord Jesus, went by the wayside, if in fact it ever existed at all in that pulpit. When I first met Jack Schaap in 1983, there was precious little evidence of it at all to be found in him.

Secondly, a professed believer is to be examined to see if his life is consistent with his profession. 1 John 2:4 says, *"He that saith, I know him, and keepeth not His commandments, is a liar, and the truth is not in him."*

So, if someone professes to be a Christian and consistently conducts themselves in a manner contrary to that profession, then we should understand that having personal suspicions concerning his salvation is not a biblically unfounded response. Jack Schaap had affairs that were the subject of widespread knowledge at First Baptist Church of Hammond. A letter about one of them is said to have achieved a good deal of circulation. We must never forget that the Apostle Paul penned his epistles to the Corinthian church on the initial premise of things *"reported commonly ... among you."* (I Co. 5:1) First Baptist Church of Hammond has for many years tried to dismiss this sort of thing as "gossip," the Apostle Paul's legitimizing of worthy suspicions notwithstanding. It does not take a genius to understand that this is nothing more than one of the more classic and primary responses to dissent in any cult. It is always designed solely as a ruse to squelch criticism.

Even so, the Bobbleheads on the platform loved it when Hyles and Schaap railed against gossip. Their Bobblehead neck springs probably needed a fresh shot of WD-40 after one of those sermons, which Hyles was always willing to supply. (I think there was always a case of it at the top of the steps behind the choir .....)

So what are we to think when a person confessing Christ, much less presenting themselves in a leadership role in the church, becomes openly involved in an adulterous relationship? In the case of Jack Schaap, make that an adulterous relationship with a girl young enough to be his granddaughter. The loyalists will say that anyone can stumble, and that we are all subject to the flesh. This is true, but I would take MONUMENTAL exception to the term "stumble." The truth is that if you stumble and go over the edge, YOU WERE TOO CLOSE TO THE EDGE! I refuse to let Jack Schaap hide out in that "nobody is perfect" crowd!

This would be a good place to correct those who have mistakenly called that relationship "an affair." Are we as Christians going to allow civil and criminals statutes of morality to exceed our Christian statutes? Man's law is predicated on the understanding that a child cannot give consent. They cannot sign contracts. They cannot take out a bank loan. And of course, they cannot give consent to have sex with an adult. So when we describe a fifty-four year old man's sexual predation upon a sixteen year old girl as "an affair," we add to the crime itself by heaping a level of responsibility on the victim that belongs only on the predator.

Secondly, Jack Schaap thought that he had a magical parachute of his predecessor's design that would gently lower him safely amidst the jagged rocks of the valley below. In the summer of 2012, that parachute failed.

The I.F.B. line in response to Schaap's disgrace is that "we are all sinners." Of course we are! What they fail to see, however (make that "refuse to see") is that Jesus plainly said that THERE ARE DEGREES OF SIN! Though this is not a popular concept on the landscape of pop theology, Jesus plainly spoke of "greater sin" in John 19:11.

To be sure, there are no degrees of sin when it comes to the positional locus of guilt resulting from sin. If you try to jump the Grand Canyon on a motorcycle, there is no graduated measure of victory based on the distance by which you missed. That principle of course, for anyone with two molecules of biblical literacy to rub together, does NOT apply to the positional reality of the new birth. You either made it across the canyon, or you did not. If you did, you did it in the arms of Jesus Christ and you will have the evidence of that in the blood His pierced hands dripped upon you in transit. THAT EXPERIENCE WILL MAKE YOU A DIFFERENT PERSON! You will from that time forward reflect the qualities of Jesus Christ, though incompletely and imperfectly, to be sure, but they will be there. (Look at Galatians chapter five to get a partial list.) Gone or seriously subdued will be the old you, and the exhaustive and unsavory list of traits describing that rascal.

If one thing comes through over and over again in looking back on the personality of Jack Schaap, it was the way he dealt with his subordinates. In a word, this guy was just plain MEAN! In fact, terms like VICIOUS, DEMEANING, BERATING, AND HUMILIATING, would be entirely accurate. Schaap regularly excoriated men older than himself in staff meetings before their friends and peers. No comment directed at those who fell short of Schaap's Machiavellian standards of performance was too degrading. These dress-down sessions were often laced with tirades of vulgarity that would make locker room banter seem mild by comparison. These accounts have been brought to the author's attention by those who witnessed the tirades first hand. (See the Appendix for one of them.)

Now with someone who was as publicly prominent, speaking to assembled crowds for multiple hours a week for eleven years, you would think that there would be visible indications of that type of imbalance. We are talking perhaps as many as 3,000 sermons here, friends! Was there not so much as one sign that this man was weekly exalting himself and robbing God of the glory that He had plainly expressed was reserved for Him and ONLY FOR HIM? Did the folks of First Baptist Church of Hammond not have a Bible in which they could read of the Bible characters who had come into the presence of God and how their lives had been transformed by that experience? Did those people sitting in the pews forget that God had over and over described Himself to us as "a jealous God?"

What did you people of First Baptist Church of Hammond think when you read I Peter 5:5 where all Christians are told to be "clothed with humility?" Could you people not see that the bravado, maniacal ego, and self-exaltation of Jack Schaap was the POLAR OPPOSITE of humility? Were 2,000+ sermons in which Schaap was the hero of every story not enough for you to understand that the man was bereft of humility? Were the three hundred plus self-references in a typical Hyles sermon compared to a tiny handful for Christ not enough to raise even a tiny red flag for you people back in that day?

Not only was this not enough then or now, but anyone who did have the courage and biblical understanding to raise that flag was pounced upon like a pack of enraged and threatened Hyenas protecting their territory from the smallest of intruders.

Now let us look at the verses that I believe speak volumes on the subject of the salvation of Jack Schaap:

"But the fruit of the Spirit is love, joy, peace, longsuffering, gentleness, goodness, faith, Meekness, temperance."
Galatians 5:21-24

"But fornication, and all uncleanness, or covetousness, let it not be once named among you, as becometh saints;"
Ephesians 5:3

This is all so simple that it just about writes itself: **THESE TRAITS WERE NOT MANIFEST IN JACK SCHAAP!** How could anyone fail to see that? There is for some, a pathetic irony and glaring hypocrisy here: carrying a Bible under one's arm to church, hearing a man like Jack Schaap use the pulpit to elevate himself at the expense of others every week and not seeing a problem. That problem is the obvious and egregious insult to a holy God who has declared that He will not share His glory with another. This is in retrospect INCOMPREHENSIBLE to the rational mind observing Jack Schaap for eleven years.

The Bible deals directly with men who prostitute their calling in Christian leadership, drawing a clear and distinct conclusion concerning their salvation:

"And many shall follow their pernicious ways; by reason of whom the way of truth shall be evil spoken of. And through covetousness shall they with feigned words make merchandise of you: whose judgment now of a long time lingereth not, and their damnation slumbereth not."
2 Peter 2:2-4

This is a description of a predator who brings reproach and shame upon the name of Jesus Christ. Men like these are labeled as liars by Peter, as he expresses how their flock is nothing more to them than "merchandise." Peter says that their judgment and damnation is surely coming.

This kind of vicious behavior was on display regularly in the life of Jack Schaap. His predation obliterated any love he may have ever had for his flock (a questionable premise itself.) Where was the "love" in destroying a seventy year old man in a staff meeting because he had not produced the numbers? Where was the "meekness" in a pulpit oratory and a homiletical style that became known primarily for chronic, screaming and shrill rants ? How could the sexual obsession of man so filled with lust and presumably pornography that even Bible reading and the Lord's Supper were described by him in sexual terms? Is this what *"becometh saints?"* How can anyone fail to understand that a man claiming to represent God who tells a mother that her young child who soils his pants in school is doing so as a sexual expression is a man with a depraved mind?

The case concerning the salvation of Jack Schaap is for me compelling. This is what God says about such individuals:

"For this ye know, that no whoremonger, nor unclean person, nor covetous man, who is an idolater, hath any inheritance in the kingdom of Christ and of God."
(Ephesians 5:5)

So then, is Jack Schaap a "whoremonger?" Does a man have to solicit prostitutes to be a whoremonger? Why don't we let the Scriptures speak for themselves on this matter.

The word "whoremonger" occurs not only in Ephesians but also in Hebrews and Revelation:

"Marriage is honourable in all, and the bed undefiled: but whoremongers and adulterers God will judge."
Hebrews 13:4

"For without are dogs, and sorcerers, and whoremongers, and murderers, and idolaters, and whosoever loveth and maketh a lie."
Revelation 22:15

"Whosoever transgresseth, and abideth not in the doctrine of Christ, hath not God. He that abideth in the doctrine of Christ, he hath both the Father and the Son."
II John 9

In Ephesians 5:5, the word "whoremonger" is the exact same Greek word: *"piprasko."* This word conveys the following meaning: "entirely under the control of the love of sinning." *(Enhanced Strong's Lexicon)* It is not describing the broken man who is debilitated and crushed, overflowing with godly sorrow over his impromptu foray into sexual sin. We find further evidence that the term describes a lifestyle of premeditated dalliances when we examine the grammatical nature of the word "whoremonger.": it is a Greek present participle, often called a "verbal noun."; in other words, the

English equivalent would end in "ing." All of this denotes continuing action. ("whoremonger-ing, describing a lifestyle, not a slip.")

In Hebrews 13:4 and Revelation 22:15, the word is the Greek term *"pornos."* This an even stronger term that refers to the practice of prostituting one's body for hire. The base of that word is the Greek word described in the preceding paragraph.

Another interesting word found in Revelation 22:15 is the word "dogs." This is the word *"kuon"* and it has a particularly interesting meaning and application when we think of a man like Jack Schaap. Here is the meaning from Strong's Greek Lexicon: *"metaphor for a man of impure mind."* How far down the river of denial does a person have to drift before they come face to face with the reality that this is a fitting description of Jack Schaap? We see plainly here that such a man belongs without the body of believers, and not among them. God likens such a man to "sorcerers", a term describing those practicing demonic arts. We also see that the whoremonger is listed alongside the murderer, a crime against God that constituted a capital offense not only then, but today as well according to the current validity given the Law in Romans chapter seven.

So the entirety of the biblically founded task at hand for us in an effort to answer the question presented as the title of this chapter now becomes clear: **Were the transgressions of Jack Schaap a "slip" into sin, or were they representative of a lifestyle?** Every person is of course free to draw their own conclusion. That being said, nobody is entitled to his own personal set of facts.

Many Christians believe that they are "playing God" in judging for themselves whether someone is in fact a Christian or not. I do not share that view, although I understand the reluctance of some to move in this direction. In the end, these judgments are like any other: their soundness and the right to make them is determined by the authority of the Scriptures on which they stand. It may be difficult to find one of those verses that so simply and convincingly expresses the criterion by which a judgement concerning the salvation of any person can rest as this one:

"He that loveth not knoweth not God."
1 John 4:8

Rather than to devote the ink and space that would be required to properly exegete Bible love, I will for the purposes at hand here express it in two words: **Jesus Christ**. God tells us that His only begotten Son was both the very definition of love as well as its highest expression. Therefore, I would ask every reader to ask themselves this question and to answer it honestly: <u>When you looked at Jack Schaap, did you think of Jesus Christ?</u>

For anyone who knew Jack Schaap, or even knew of him from those who knew him or were close to him, the only question that needs to be asked concerning whether or not he was a Christian is a very simple and obvious one: DID JACK SCHAAP REFLECT THE QUALITIES OF JESUS CHRIST? Did he follow Peter's admonition to *"feed the flock of God"* or did he feed ON the flock of God? Did Schaap follow the command in that same passage (I Peter 5), *"Being examples to the flock?"* Sadly, in the end "the emperor had no clothes," only this time, Hans Christian Andersen's tale found its literal expression.

"And hereby we do know that we know him, if we keep his commandments. He that saith, I know him, and keepeth not his commandments, is a liar, and the truth is not in him."
1 John 2:3-6

114

With every bit of objectivity, honesty and fairness, when I look at the facts and shine upon them the light of biblical judgment indicated in all these verses above, I feel a strong current leading me in the direction of a personal conclusion regarding the salvation of Jack Schaap. I have not for many years ventured beyond the framing of this subject in this manner. If the man is not a Christian, that proclamation of John's above will stand between him and the credibility of his genuine salvation. Some will say that the fact that he has been so severely judged and punished is evidence of his salvation. I can make no authoritative argument against that possibility.

My position then for many years was that I did not believe that Jack Schaap to be a saved man. It has been very interesting for me to see some of the best Christians I know and to whom I have gone to do the "iron sharpeneth iron" directive on this subject, come down on both sides of this issue. However, my reluctance to come right out and say all changed for me on the evening of September 22, 2012.

My wife and I had just come back from a delightful drive up around Possum Kingdom Lake in North Texas. I have a fun little red roadster in which we enjoyed having the top down under a cloudless blue sky. We ate lunch in a lovely and elegant resort perched high upon the cliffs of Possum Kingdom Lake.

When we came home, I watched a very recent video of Jack Schaap. He was not preaching and he was not in a pulpit. At one point in the video he was talking about himself. And then, there it was: a statement that I knew would change everything concerning my view of the man's salvation. With that utterance from the man's own mouth I would go from a position of leaning toward doubting his salvation to being 99.9% convinced that Jack Schaap had never truly become a Christian. After giving this careful thought, I recalled that this was not the first time I had ever heard him say the words I heard that evening.

I wanted to proceed very cautiously in my thoughts. I am exceedingly blessed to have one man in this world who is my "go to" man on matters of doctrine and on the finer points of Systematic Theology. He is my now retired first pastor, Pastor Dorman Owens. I have often called him "a walking encyclopedia of doctrine." Any time in my Christian life that I have found myself to be even moderately in disagreement with Pastor Dorman, my immediate reaction has always been to assume that I am wrong, and that a careful study of the matter will prove him right. That is not elevating a man beyond a proper level, nor should it be seen as an expression of humility on my part. It is just what I have come to see as the proper and rational way to proceed after knowing this eighty year old man for thirty years.

So I got my mentor and friend, Pastor Dorman, on the phone and asked him if he would draw the same conclusion about Jack Schaap's salvation as I did after hearing what he had said. He told me unquestionably that he would. Not only that, but he steered me to the Scriptures that turned my initial presumption into a solid, biblically based and very firm conclusion for me.

Jack Schaap said publicly the month before his arrest that had "been saved when I was five years old." I remembered him telling me long ago when we were friends that his sister had led him to the Lord. She was not much older than he was. I do not know of anyone who has ever heard of Jack Schaap talking about a re-affirmation event later in his life concerning his salvation experience at age five. Neither do I know of any Christian, pastor, conference leader, editor, Christian author, evangelist, professor or Bible teacher who has ever questioned the salvation experience of a pastor with a church membership of 15,000 when that profession was made at age five. That is POSITIVELY ASTOUNDING to me!

I would like to shine the light of the Christian Scriptures on a salvation experience claimed to have occurred at age five. Is it possible for a child of five to be saved? Can a five year old understand the elements of salvation and make a responsible decision concerning the fate of his or her eternal soul? Does a five year old have the capacity to offend God unto damnation? Does a five year old child go to hell when he dies? Interesting questions all.

I believe that we have to go to the Apostle Paul's writings to the church at Rome, as Pastor Dorman led me to see. When we do, this matter will become abundantly clear for us there and these questions will be answered. Here are the verses at play for us here. I believe that a solid and fair exegesis of these verses will tell us all what we need to know about whether a five year old child can be spiritually redeemed or even needs to be.

" Wherefore, my brethren, ye also are become dead to the law by the body of Christ; that ye should be married to another, even to him who is raised from the dead, that we should bring forth fruit unto God."

"For when we were in the flesh, the motions of sins, which were by the law, did work in our members to bring forth fruit unto death."

"But now we are delivered from the law, that being dead wherein we were held; that we should serve in newness of spirit, and not in the oldness of the letter. What shall we say then? Is the law sin? God forbid. Nay, I had not known sin, but by the law: for I had not known lust, except the law had said, Thou shalt not covet."

"But sin, taking occasion by the commandment, wrought in me all manner of concupiscence. For without the law sin was dead."

"For I was alive without the law once: but when the commandment came, sin revived, and I died. And the commandment, which was ordained to life, I found to be unto death."

"For sin, taking occasion by the commandment, deceived me, and by it slew me."
Romans 7:4-11

First of all, we have to ask ourselves if a five year old child is under the condemnation of the law. This is a purely Catholic doctrine. Roman Catholics believe, based on Romans 5:12, *("Wherefore, as by one man sin entered into the world, and death by sin; and so death passed upon all men, for that all have sinned:")* that children are born guilty and go to Hell if they die before being saved through the church.

Note that Paul says in verse seven above that were are *"become dead to the Law by the body of Christ."* So then are we to believe that a four year old is under the condemnation of the Law? If he dies as a four year old, he or she burns in Hell forever? Really? Does a small child barely out of diapers *"bring fruit unto death?"* Try looking at a baby in a stroller some day as his adoring young mother wheels him through the park and say, "Oh look at him! Isn't he precious, all cozy in that blanket, bringing fruit unto death."

Does a baby need to be *"delivered from the law?"* Doesn't he or she maybe need to UNDERSTAND the law first? Is a baby really being "held" by the Law? How is he or she confined to the *"oldness of the letter?"*

Can we imagine a conversation with a five year old (with another child no less) where the slightly older child tries to explain to them how they *"had not known lust but by the law."* Really? With their eternal soul at stake, a five year old child can be expected to come to an understanding of those matters, process them, and make the most important decision of their life? REALLY?

Now it all gets even more problematic for someone trying to make the case for a five year old's salvation. Those who believe a five year old can make that decision, please explain to me how that child's lifetime of sin has *"wrought in me all manner of concupiscence."* (Romans 7:8) Really? At age five a child has not left any stone unturned in experienceing every kind of sin and evil under the sun? Mom, with all due respect, please allow me to suggest that you need to keep an eye on that kind of kid between the time you tuck him in at night and when he wakes up in the morning!

How much sin is there in a five year old to make the moment when "sin revived" the moment when spiritual death was pronounced upon a child? Does a five year old child have the capacity to understand the concept that Paul was bringing out in verse ten concerning the Law bringing spiritually fatal levels of guilt when properly understood? Can a five year old then really confess that his sin *"taking occasion by the commandment, deceived me, and by it slew me?"*

Lastly, I would ask you, the reader, some pointed questions:

- If a five year old child is old enough to be saved, isn't he old enough to be condemned to Hell?

- Is the God we serve a God who would do that?

- Has any man stood before a tiny casket and believed that the soul that once lived in that child's body now burns in hell?

119

• Is the age of accountability less than five?

Sorry, but I believe that a five year old has no concept of genuine biblical redemption. Can he repeat a prayer? Yes. Does he want "Jesus in his heart?" Yes. Does he want to make Mom and dad happy and get bragged on in church? Yes. Does he want to be baptized like a big boy? Yes. Can he be made afraid of burning in Hell? Yes. Would I trust my salvation to an experience as a five year old? NEVER IN A MILLION YEARS!

Whatever the case may be concerning the state and eternal future of Jack Schaap's soul, I can only hope that he humbles himself before a holy God and finds redemption, lest he one day hears a sentence pronounced upon him that will make his prison sentence seem pale in comparison:

"I never knew you: depart from me,
ye that work iniquity."
Matthew 7:23

Chapter

13

James On Jack

The goal of every Christian when it comes to sin is very simple: <u>see it as God sees it</u>. A very practical reason for this is that this is ultimately the perspective from which we will be held accountable for our lives. To believe otherwise is to rely on a very problematic, shaky and ill-advised premise: the belief that the Bible is not true. Simply put in light of the empirical evidence to the contrary, this is a bad bet.

I have discussed this subject with many people and I have yet to met a single person whose rejection of the Judaeo-Christian Scriptures as morally authoritative was not based on the same personal agenda: a desire for moral sovereignty over their own lives. People with this agenda always understand that the Bible lies squarely in that path of that autonomy and must be moved out of the way at any cost, and irrespective of any empirical evidence as to its accuracy. The Apostle John called this, ***"the record that God gave of his Son."*** (I John 5:10)

Never have I seen that task undertaken, much less successfully completed without that overwhelmingly evident motivation. It never works. You can fool the brain, but there is a part of us that cannot be fooled as easily. That part can only be ignored or silenced. The clinical term is "Cognitive Dissonance," the clinical method by which a person successfully lies to themselves. We humans are quite good at it. Moral anarchists are masters.

With that in mind, I would like to examine a few brief verses from Scripture that I believe perfectly describe the dynamics and events in the fall of Jack Schaap. They are from the first chapter of the book of James, a book that is sometimes referred to as "The Book of Proverbs of the New Testament."These verses emerge as having enormous significance and relevance in understanding the fall of men like Jack Schaap. They describe, in what you will see is amazing detail, every aspect of that kind of fall from grace. It is for me like being back in my ski racing and days watching a post-disaster slow motion video of one of my high speed falls in a ski race with an astute coach at my side. Often you can see that a fall did not just happen, but that mistakes in balance, weight distribution, angulation and timing were made long before the fall occurred. They then compounded each other to create what the casual observer would think just happened all of a sudden. That is rarely the case in ski racing. At higher speeds like a 90 mile per hour downhill race, these mistakes keep a racer from properly resisting every ski racer's great enemy: centrifugal force. This is the force that tries to pull every racer off course on every turn. At these speeds, it is a formidable oponent and when it wins, the falls are seldom anything short of spectacular. I can tell you one other thing about these falls: they hurt!

"But every man is tempted, when he is
drawn away of his own lust, and enticed. Then when
lust hath conceived, It bringeth forth sin: and sin,
when it is finished, bringeth forth death."

"If any man among you seem to be religious, and
bridleth not his tongue, but deceiveth his own heart,
this man's religion is vain."
James 1:14-15, & 26

There are five steps listed here that take a Christian from a position of stability and respect in the Christian life to the ultimate disgrace of moral failure:

1. A man is DRAWN AWAY by his own lust
2. That man is then TEMPTED.
3. That man is then ENTICED by the temptation.
4. The accompanying lust brings SIN into the man's life.
5. That sin leads to DEATH.

I would like to put these verses under the microscope of sound biblical analysis and the proper exegesis to which this leads the serious student of God's Word. I have learned that this requires an understanding of the language in which these verses were originally presented: the Koine Greek of the New Testament, a powerful and precise language that is far superior and considerably more descriptive than our English of today. I have often said that this language compared to our English is like having on a surgical glove as opposed to a ski mitten and trying to pick up a dime off a table.

What does it mean to be *"drawn away of his own lust?"* The word at the heart of that concept that James uses here is the Greek word *"exelko."* Allow me to share the definition of this very descriptive term as it is expressed in metaphor in the Greek Lexicon: *"to lure forth: in hunting and fishing as game is lured from its hiding place, so man by lure is al<u>lured</u> from the safety of self-restraint to sin."*

For the last dozen years or so I have fished often. We lived on a thirteen acre wildlife preserve in Northwest Indiana and we built our own lake as well as several ponds. It was a beautiful setting with a large waterfall, a fountain, a sand beach and a large dock. Those waters were stocked with Bass, Bluegill, and Catfish. Rarely did I venture through a large store without looking to see if they had a fishing section. When they did, there was always one main draw for me: lures. Lures have come a long way since I was a kid fishing on the shores of Lake Champlain or on the shores of the Mediterranean in the South of France. Today the movement of high quality lures in the water is at least for me, impossible to distinguish from the swimming of a real fish. I remember saying at times when I was on our dock trying out a new lure in the clear waters of our lake, "How can a hungry Bass resist that?"

What I was essentially doing was trying to deceive the fish. What is interesting is that this was all about the sporting aspect of the experience, not catching dinner. If it was all about just reaching the goal of catching a big Bass, I would have slipped into the water with my spear gun, picked out the best looking fish, taken aim and pulled the trigger at close range. I learned to spearfish from the Tahitians, the best in the world at this art. The fact is, fish do not fear divers and this sometimes makes spear fishing too easy.

What I was doing to the prized Largemouth Bass in our lake was taking advantage of their hunger. I was only successful, as any fisherman, when their hunger was the principal factor in their decision to go after my <u>alluring</u> representation of their food source. Much depended on the luremaker's skill. With the combination of a hungry Bass and the right movement in a lure, that Bass had a meeting with my camera dockside, and yes, occasionally my wife's frying pan.

This is an apt, if not a perfect narrative of what takes place when a man is attracted to a woman other than his wife. Solomon warned his sons at great length of these dangers of life. He told them to ***"keep thy heart with all diligence."*** Understanding that the eyegate was what made the lure work for men, he told them to ***"Let thine eyes look right on and let thine eyelids look straight before thee."***

Eyelids signify closed eyes, so the reference to eyelids was perhaps a reference to what we see with the eyes closed—often what some fantasize about in the privacy of their thoughts.

Solomon got much more specific in this discussion from Proverbs in chapters three and four in warning his sons about morally loose women: *"Remove thy way far from her and come not nigh the door of her house."* In other words: "STAY OUT OF THAT NEIGHBORHOOD, boys!" The reason is that the stage needs to be set for someone's lust to overpower their judgment, and there are some places that facilitate that process more than others. It is part of the "perfect storm." Once that stage is set, then the second phase of the capture that James describes can take place.

Pornography is for many men today, the place to which they can be "drawn away." I have dedicated a previous chapter to that, and to the impact I believe it had on Jack Schaap. I believe that Jack Schaap came to the place where he could not see a woman as anything other than a sexual object. I believe that the man was so full of the cancer of pornography that it came out regularly in much of what he spoke from the pulpit. Just as the food we have eaten stays on our breath, Jack Schaap could not help but exude what he had taken in. Consider some of the things he said from the pulpit:

- "You can sing Amazing Grace sexually. I have heard it done."

- "There are some female entertainers that can get you pretty aroused while you are listening to them sing about the grace of God."

- Described Purdue co-eds: "Girls in their fishnet with no underclothing."

- "The person who deeply loves Christ understands that

when he receives Christ as savior, it is spiritual intercourse."

• "Communion is an act of spiritual intercourse."

• Describing the Psalmist's phrase "laid before me" he taught that David's relationship with the Word of God was a sexual metaphor.

• He talked jokingly about how if he thought it would help he would "send my wife up to the South Side of Chicago (known for prostitution) "in a miniskirt and a fur coat in the back seat of a Cadillac" to raise the money for which they had become so desperate to pay for the new thirty million dollar auditorium, Schaap's grandiose and ill-advised monument to himself.

I have heard this kind of language from a pulpit twice in my Christian life. The first time was while attending Liberty Baptist Church in Lake Station, Indiana. Pastor Bill Beith regularly used very coarse language from the pulpit. My wife was uncomfortable with this practice. I went to see Beith about it. He answered me, "People hear way worse than that on television." Not long after that, his name was plastered as front page headlines in the Northwest Indiana newspapers. Pastor Beith pleaded guilty to exposing himself to a MALE undercover police officer and soliciting that man for oral sex. The church ignored what one man knew to be inappropriate at Liberty Baptist Church: vulgar pulpit talk. They ignored it at their own peril. That church has now been boarded up for years.

Bill Beith was also neck-deep in pornography. An evangelist friend of mine saw him walking out of an X-rated movie theater in Chicago Heights, Illinois. He confronted Beith, who at first said he only went in to find out the time. When pressed, Beith admitted otherwise. Later, I hired a private investigator and found out that Pastor Beith was a regular in strip clubs throughout the area.

At First Baptist Church of Hammond in August of 2012, this pattern of sexually charged expressions from the pulpit produced the same result.

The word "enticed" used in the verses above by James is the Greek word *"deleazo,"* which comes from a primary word that means "decoy." A decoy, quite obviously is to hunting what a lure is to fishing. It is meant to mimic and fool an animal by appealing to his appetite rather than his judgment.

The water in our lake was exceptionally clear, so I was able to see the reaction of fish to various lures. Over time, one thing became very evident: it was the younger, less mature fish that were the most easily fooled by my lures. The larger, older Bass would not so much as swim up to a lure to examine it; neither were they interested in my synthetic "Powerbaits," that looked, moved and supposedly tasted just like a real worm. There was a "Grandpa Bass" out there, but he was never too interested in my lures. He came for the free fish food we threw in, but he could spot a lure from a long way off. Jack Schaap's belief was that he could get the worm and spit out the hook. He was wrong.

After the enticement comes the TEMPTATION. The word "tempted" is the Greek word *"peirazo."* In the context of this verse, we see a very interesting dynamic that presents itself in the behavior of men like Jack Schaap. I have described this before in these pages in the reasonings of Schaap's predecessor and mentor, Jack Hyles. Hyles literally thought himself so indispensable to God that he could harbor in his heart both an illicit relationship and a devotion to the cause of Christ. I have called that the "Samson Syndrome." This is key to understanding the deeper meaning and correct biblical context of temptation.

One of the definitions of temptation is "to try or test one's faith, virtue, character, by enticement to sin." What this expresses is quite interesting. This is a person saying, "I can take this lust into my bosom and not be burned." The foolishness of that thought was expressed rhetorically by Solomon:

> *"Can a man take fire in his bosom,*
> *... and not be burned?"*
> Proverbs 6:27

I am convinced beyond any shadow of doubt that Jack Schaap's answer to Solomon's rhetorical question was a resounding and prideful "<u>YES!</u>" Not only that, but I am also convinced beyond any element of doubt that Jack Schaap felt entitled to his dual life. He believed he could manage it all. He believed that he could successfully compartmentalize his life. He never expected a bit of trouble in executing that lifestyle. That immense pride brought him to a level of carelessness that proved to be his eventual downfall. Like all dictators, he had never cultivated the capacity to deny himself anything he wanted.

One of the definitions of the word used by James for temptation is the following: *"impious or wicked conduct to test God's justice and patience, and to challenge Him [God]; as it were to give proof of His perfections."* The interesting and highly relevant element here is the challenge to God. I don't know if this is a direct, primary and perfect fit, for I have not been able to delve into the minds of the two Jacks that deeply. What I have done is to draw reasonable and what I believe to be sound conclusions based on the overwhelming body of evidence. However, if there is not an explicit, THERE IS AN IMPLICIT CHALLENGE HERE TO GOD. The challenge is that in the face of sixty-six Bible books delineating Christian conduct and moral virtue in great detail, a man could boldly claim executive moral privilege and by his actions express that he is entitled to the transgressions forbidden to everyone else, even the ones that God thought worthy of the death penalty.

Then James says that a big part of this cause-and-effect chain of events is LUST. This is the Greek word *"epithumia."* This is defined as desire for what is forbidden. It comes from a root word that is defined as *"the wine of passion."* In other words, lust is seen by the writer as an intoxicant. Any one knows that to be under the influence of an intoxicant is to have one's judgment seriously compromised. This is why Solomon understood that intoxicants were *"not for kings."* They can bring about a slip from a great height that leaves the climber not just on a lower level, but in the valley floor, often crippled for life and without hope of ever again enjoying the view from the summit. Is this not Jack Schaap today?

The word used also is defined as a *"craving for what is forbidden."* Jack Schaap didn't just go out of bounds, he allowed himself the personal privilege of entirely redefining that boundary for himself. Sadly, his cleat marks will be forever visible in the white chalk lines that define a godly life, and the points he scored downfield have been unceremoniously taken off the scoreboard.

This lust then conceives, James tells us. James chooses the Greek word *"sullambano."* The meaning is simple and powerful, an oh so accurate to describe the fall of Jack Schaap: *"to seize, take one as prisoner."* It reminds me of the term biblical term "snare," and how it is distinguished from the term "trap" by being a device intended to capture its prey alive. This is when one feels the searing pain in the bosom implied in Solomon's rhetorical question given above. That pain can continue for the adulterous spouse for the rest of their lives.

Is there redemption? Can there be forgiveness? Is God not "faithful and just to forgive" sinners? Yes He is, just like you and I would hopefully forgive those who had sinned against us <u>if they sought that forgiveness through the proper biblical protocol</u>. Once you steal money, however, don't expect to be elected church treasurer. Once you molest a child, don't expect to be a youth worker. The qualifications for a shepherd in the New Testament church are best expressed in two biblical words: ***"beyond reproach."***

The conception in the above paragraphs gives birth to the act that thus far has been approached, contemplated, fantasized about, and acted out in the mind. Once actualized, those things become action. This is the emergence of sin, and the point of no return. It is defined as, *"to miss or wander from the path of uprightness and honour, to do or go wrong; to wander from the law of God, violate God's law..."*

I remember that in our long crossings of Lake Michigan aboard our sailboat, Renaissance, an error of only one degree or less at the onset of the trip would mean that we would miss our port on the other side of the sixty-eight mile crossing by several miles. This was enormously serious if we happened to be coming in at one a.m. in the dark of night and in the midst of a storm. Jack Schaap had plenty of opportunities for a course correction in the months and years before his fall. I will print in the appendix one of those opportunities that came from me. Many others penned letters of this nature from their hearts, seeing the dangers that lay ahead for a man they had once respected, and in cases like mine, with whom they had been close friends. He never acknowledged one of those letters.

Then comes death, James tells us. The word of choice for James is *"thanatos"*. Here is how it that word is defined in this usage: *"in the widest sense, death comprising all the miseries arising from sin, as well physical death as the loss of a life consecrated to God and blessed in him on earth."*

A secondary meaning is *"to make filthy, befoul, to defile, dishonour."*

Sin is not merely a spontaneous act, but the result of a long process that I have attempted to present here. The words used by James liken the process to physical conception and birth. James personifies this chain of events and shows that it can follow a similar sequence and produce sin with all of its deadly results. While sin does not result in spiritual death for the genuine believer, it surely can lead to physical death as related to Christians by the Apostle Paul. (1 Cor. 11:30; 1 John 5:16).

After the myriad of similar sins that have been swept under the rug at First Baptist Church of Hammond, finally there is one that wouldn't fit. It did not matter how high the enablers lifted the carpet and how frantically the sweepers plied their well learned craft. The carpet was full, the dust cloud was too noxious, and the stench was beyond covering up.

Finally, in the end, the lesson that may emerge with the most value, and sadly the greatest cost, may be the advice Jack Schaap gave to others and failed to heed himself:

"You boys who want to win the world to Christ, keep your zipper up."
Jack Schaap

*"Hyles had to, at all cost,
keep his people from thinking
independently. His invention of
'Blind Loyalty' served that
purpose admirably."*

Chapter

14

Paul On Jack

Jack Hyles was death on gossip. He had to be. The only problem was, like everything else the man put out, he never presented things on a solid biblical foundation. The same was true of gossip. Hyles and Schaap had a great need to keep people from disagreeing with them.

Hyles had to at all cost keep his people from thinking independently and from generating the slightest critical momentum in the church. His invention of "Blind Loyalty" served that purpose admirably. Hyles even had complete veto power over the appointment of any deacon whom he felt had not signed on to this bizarre concept. When the names of deacon candidates at First Baptist Church of Hammond were presented to the deacon board for a final vote, Hyles would always ask the men to bow their heads and close their eyes. Then he would say that if anyone knew of any reason why the man whose name he had just read was not deacon material, they should quietly (and secretly) slip their hand up. Of course, if Hyles did not think that the candidate had drunk sufficiently or deeply enough of the Kool-Aid, nothing prevented him from pretending that a hand had been raised, since no one was looking but him. How convenient....and brilliant!

Nobody in Hyles' church had ever given any thought to the evident fact that the entire epistles to the Corinthian church penned by the Apostle Paul had been motivated by what Hyles would have himself called gossip:

"It is reported commonly that there is fornication among you."
1 Corinthians 5:1

"For first of all, when ye come together in the church, I hear that there be divisions among you; and I partly believe it. For there must be also heresies among you, that they which are approved may be made manifest among you."
1 Corinthians 11:18-19

Thank God that Paul did not adopt the classic cult method of labeling the whistleblowers from the Corinth church as "malcontents." Paul understood that a major element of the authority in the New Testament church resided IN THE MEMBERSHIP. According to the Hyles doctrine, however, Paul had "DIED SPIRITUALLY" by the mere act of listening to concerned members of the church at Corinth! In fact, the Apostle Paul went further: HE CONCLUDED THAT THERE WAS HERETICAL DOCTRINE BEING TAUGHT IN THE CORINTH CHURCH! He said that plainly in verse 19 above.

Paul was by Hyles' definition, spurred to write his letters to the church at Corinth because he had listened to gossip! There were many things "reported commonly" in the Hammond church. Rather than to consider the possibility that where there was so much smoke, there may in fact be a fire, Hyles' constant admonitions were always the same: IGNORE THE SMOKE!

Paul made plain to the church at Corinth that what had been "reported commonly" in fact had merit. The same was true about Jack Hyles, Jack Schaap and their merry band of fornicators some two thousand years later:

"I...could not speak unto you as unto spiritual, but as unto carnal."
1 Corinthians 3:1

Paul took the sin of fornication more seriously than we can imagine. Many Christians today falsely believe the Old Testament Law was done away with in the New Testament. Paul did not believe anything like that. He wrote plainly that the Law was valid after Christ:

"Wherefore the law is holy, and the commandment holy, and just, and good."
Romans 7:12

We must also never lose sight of the severity of the punishment that God had ordained for sexual sins: DEATH! (Deuteronomy 22:22) Does grace and mercy moderate that in New Testament times? Of course, but we would do well to remember that God still believed that violators DESERVED the death penalty for Old Testament capital offenses. That is why Paul was able to convey the seriousness of God's view of fornication:

"Know ye not that ye are the temple of God, and that the Spirit of God dwelleth in you? If any man defile the temple of God, him shall God destroy; for the temple of God is holy, which temple ye are."
Corinthians 3:16-17

The word "destroy" that Paul uses here is the Greek word *phtheiro*, which comes from a root word meaning "to waste." This harkens back to the view that Jews had of the manner in which the Jewish temple had been defiled by heathens such as the Babylonians, and later Roman conquerors. In the opinion of the Jews, this was no different from a physical destruction. The end result was identical: the temple could no longer be used for its intended purposes.

As I was putting the finishing touches on this book, Jack Schaap signed a plea agreement in the federal court in Hammond, Indiana. The U.S. Attorney announced that Schaap signed a plea agreement admitting he took a minor across state lines with the intent to engage in sexual activity. Jack Schaap would never again be used for the intended purpose that God had at one time ordained for him.

On July 20th, 1985, Jack Schaap signed our marriage certificate. On my birthday in 2012, he signed his name to a plea agreement prepared by TWO WOMEN US Attorneys. He once thundered from the pulpit that he was not going to take advice on theology from any woman. Perhaps not, but in a stunning and surely purposeful crafting of an irony so piquant and delicious to the thousands of women he had berated, humiliated and abused for eleven years, it was in the end two women, Assistant US Attorneys Jill Koster and Susan Collins who finally brought Jack Schaap to his knees.

Chapter

15

Don't Throw The Baby Out With The Bath Water

Sometimes people become the thing they despise. I have in my lifetime often seen black folks display incredibly vicious levels of racism. Many of them apparently feel today that they are entitled to it because of the years of persecution. I am not one of those people. I don't think there is a more racist organization than the Black Panther Party. They are Black Supremacists, plain and simple, and they make no pretense of disguise.

I have seen the same thing play out with many people who left the Independent Fundamental Baptist Movement. In no way do I want to minimize either, slavery, institutional racism and segregation, or ecclesiastical abuse at the hands of the I.F.B. Movement. However, I have come to believe that overreaction to abuse can be as bad as no reaction.

I don't think there are very many people who have been more vocal than I have in their criticism and exposition of the endemic abuse in the Independent Fundamental Baptist

Movement. I can count those that have on one hand and have fingers left over. Still, there will be those for whom anyone driving within a block of an I.F.B. church will be unceremoniously pounced upon. That being said, it is impossible for me to publicly demonstrate in the slightest of ways that I have never been willing to throw the baby out with the bath water without an immediate formation of a circular firing squad by those whose hearts have become filled with hatred.

God seems to have placed the qualification for a "remnant" at one percent. I have spoken to Walter E. Rast, one of the archaeologists who excavated Sodom and Gomorrah. He tells me that the city population was around 1,000. That would place the ten righteous men indicated in the account for which God would spare the city at one percent. Is it realistic to hold out hope that one percent of the Independent Fundamental Baptist Movement is sound and sees the sin in the camp as God sees it? The sad truth is that although I hold out hope, I am personally reluctant to make that assumption.

There is something peculiar about the human race, in that we so often find a way to become like those we dislike the most. As I have pointed out, Hyles became more Catholic in his church polity than anyone ever realized, especially the man himself. For many who read this book, the mention of this evokes the same response it did in 1989: "What six hundred pound gorilla in the room?"

Some who have emerged from First Baptist Church of Hammond and Hyles-Anderson College, may have today thrown the baby out with the bath water. No Christian group has ever been 100% right or 100% wrong in what they professed. The responsibility for *"rightly dividing the word of truth"* is an individual responsibility, not a corporate mandate.

Jack Hyles was against homosexuality; he was right. Moses,

the principal author of the Old Testament called it an *"abomination."* The principle author of the New Testament, the Apostle Paul, called it *"vile affections."* Today, you will find in the Internet forums established by and for the victims of I.F.B. abuse, a number of people supporting a tolerance for homosexuality and a solidarity with the advocates of that lifestyle. That is throwing the baby out with the bath water. These forums themselves sometimes seem to turn into "circular firing squads."

Jack Hyles was also right in some other areas. Few men are ever 100% wrong. Most cults have foundational and practical elements that are correct. <u>That is what allows them to camouflage their error and deceit</u>. To overreact to a cult dynamic and toss out everything about them is always a practice fraught with danger. Sadly, there are thousands of former members of Independent Fundamental Baptist Churches who now solidly espouse the complete spectrum of beliefs that today define Secular Humanism.

At some point, you have to stop running from the bear, or eventually you will go off a cliff. I am all for distancing myself from any predator in the woods, but there does come a time when I am no longer willing to allow that escape to define who I am and how I see every single element of the world around me. I have very little patience or respect for anyone who continues to be a part of the corrupt elements of the I.F.B. system, but I don't hate them. I was deceived for six years. Why in the world would I ever want to now give them that kind of control over me? The I.F.B. boogeyman is real to me, but I refuse to see one behind every single tree in the forest. There are still some good Baptist preachers out there. When you find the perfect church, here is how you will know it: it will have a driveway made of transparent gold.

I have been on many dives in the oceans of the world. On numerous occasions we would see marine creatures big enough to do some real damage to a diver. Every time we saw a large shark, (we measured them in girth, not length so as not to scare folks later) there would always be someone in the dive group that spent the rest of the dive looking over his shoulder. Often we would have to curtail the dive for the rest of the dive party because that person whose fear defined their dive would run out of air way before everyone else. That was so senseless to me, as it deprived all of us of the beauty of a dive on a coral reef with sunlit visibility in the 150 foot range, often even more. I called those dives the closest thing to visiting another planet, and I thought it tragic to curtail even one because fear had defined the experience of one diver.

Equally senseless is to allow one's heart to be filled with so much hatred that the hatred begins to define you. It begins to control you. It begins to monopolize more and more of your time. You begin to gravitate toward others who have that same hatred. You develop less and less tolerance for others who have reacted differently to the abuse in their lives that is similar to what you experienced. Maybe they have stabilized on the level of disdain or contempt for their abusers, or even forgiveness.

Many people will lump others into the abuser group if they are not willing to unconditionally denounce the entire group, and everything they believe. Unfortunately, when it comes to the Christian faith, that baby can fly out the window with the bath water. That baby's name is often Jesus.

Chapter

16

Should I Forgive?

At the end of the day, I want focus on you, the reader, because I care about you so much more than I care about Jack Schaap or First Baptist Church of Hammond. Until the day comes when they man up and own their past, they will remain a very dark stain on the history of religion in America, and a convenient tool for the God bashers. Since I firmly believe that they will never truly repent, I am content to play my small part in turning up the light of accountability on them as bright as I can get it to go. That is all I can do, other than to counsel the victims. I have been doing that for twenty-five years.

Now in the course of healing or recovery, or whatever one feels the need to call it, there are really only two things that are important to understand:

1.) If you draw close enough to Jesus Christ, you will be made 100% whole.
2.) There is no biblical requirement for universal forgiveness, but you must cultivate a forgiving heart, ready to forgive if the biblical conditions for forgiveness are met. (This probably is more for your sake than anyone else's.)

Let us deal first with your relationship to Jesus Christ. Jesus Christ does not micro-manage man's expression and practice of religion, any more than a lofty mountain peak on the horizon is involved in deciding how you execute the journey to its base, which base camp you choose, or how you later undertake the ascent.

God put the truths of the Christian faith into the hands of man. What else was He to do? He could have made us robots, but in the end, we needed to have free choice to validate in the eyes of our Creator the measure of love we extend to Him. There has been a lot of "operator error" as organized religion succumbed repeatedly throughout history to the moral gene that underwent an unfortunate mutation many aeons ago in a beautiful and lush garden in the Tigris Euphrates Valley. We ALL have that gene.

The human race has the topographical map to the mountain's summit, and that in amazing detail. I have abundant reason to believe (and so do you), that the Judaeo-Christian Scriptures are authentic; they are what they claim to be—the Word of God. I am not an easy person to fool. I believe that I have been blessed with a respectable level of discernment. I also believe that I have been blessed in that I come from good intellectual and academic stock. I have spent twelve years in institutions of higher learning beyond the high school level. I have written twelve books. I have done my homework for three decades, and I believe the Bible is what it claims to be. It has 55,000 archaeological evidences that support it's veracity. Over 500 highly credentialed scientists from many of the most prestigious universities and research institutions worldwide believe that there is no scientific data anywhere that contradicts anything that the Bible presents. That book then makes the claim to be divinely inspired, and says of it's Author,

"In His favor is Life."
(Psalm 30:5)

142

If you listen to my testimony, you will see that I have personally validated this divine axiom in my own life. I often tell non-Christians what a foolish thing it is to bet one's eternal soul that the Bible is not true. Those doubting that always, in my experience, have a personal agenda that revolves around an intense desire to live their lives as completely free and unbound moral agents. God put it this way:

"Men loved darkness rather than light
because their deeds were evil."
(John 3:19)

I have learned never to go into any detail concerning how I have been blessed in life. Any time that I have done so in the past, it seems like there are those out there who are quick to accuse me of boasting. I have an embroidered sign on the wall in my office directly above my monitor that reads: "Count Your Blessings." I do that a lot. I wouldn't trade my life for anyone's on the planet.

So my question to those of you who sat in the same pews I did at 523 Sibley Street and at 8400 Burr Street, or any other cult church, is a simple one: **why would you hold a holy, perfect and righteous God who has directed the most incredible expression of sacrificial love in the universe to your front door accountable for the dark shadow that a few impostor-degenerates have cast upon you?**

For years I would drive around Northwest Indiana on Saturday afternoon with the top down and some good tunes playing (I like acoustic, Delta-style Blues) and enjoy the fresh air and sunshine. I loved the smell of wild onions in the Spring coming from the woods in southern Lake County, Indiana. My main purpose, however, was to find some little church tucked away on a back road somewhere, where just maybe someone would step into the pulpit on Sunday and try to be a blessing to my soul. I didn't give up easily, but it soon became apparent to me that such a church existed only in the landscape of my ecclesiastical idealism. Oh, I got off to a few good starts now and then. I saw a lovely, twinkling light at the end of the tunnel from time to time. But eventually, I would hear a discomfiting rumble and in a pall of dust, the rocks would tumble from the tunnel ceiling and I was dodging boulders once again. Before long, the light I had seen and toward which I was cautiously moving was no longer visible, and I was back in my little green roadster the following Saturday, plying the backroads of a Christian idealism that refused to die.

The rumble and ensuing tumble of rocks was usually church politics: decisions would always be made on the basis of what was deemed to be in the best interest of the church, not what would please a holy and righteous God. One pastor looked at me like I was crazy when I told him, *"You are making this decision on the basis of what is expedient for the church. Righteousness has no say in it."* He just kept repeating over and over: *"I am not going to lose ten people out of our Sunday School."*

The trouble had begun when I had offended a woman in my adult Sunday School class. She had a feminist ideology and thought that my teaching on Adam and Eve was repressive and archaic. A robust woman, she was the pastor's secretary and her father was the chairman of the deacon board. She knew how to make trouble, and that she did. I left that church in disgust. This was a shame because a young woman had come running out to our car in the parking lot the week before and said to me in my wife's presence: "Jerry, your Sunday School lessons on Adam and Eve saved our marriage. We were about to file for divorce, and now we have decided that with our new understanding of marriage, we can have the kind of marriage that will work. Thank you." My heart soared like a hawk.

Yes, I know how bad churches can be. I once sat down with the pastor of a large church in Northwest Indiana. They had been a longstanding Baptist Church. They had also seriously capitulated in doctrinal areas. He had offered to meet with any prospective member to discuss church beliefs and answer questions. I wrote him nine letters to try to take him up on that offer, and there was no response. I had him pegged as a political weasel, when I finally wrote him again and told him that if he was not going to meet with me to at least have the decency and the integrity to man up and tell me so. A few days later, I was sitting across from him in his office. To his credit, he began by apologizing for ignoring my letters.

I asked him why there were Bible subjects he never preached on, listing them one by one. He never hesitated at all to answer: "Jerry, if I ever preached on that, I'd lose ten families." What little respect I had for him went down in one big flush.

Later on, I was ever so briefly hopeful for the man when it was announced that there would be a "question and answer time" that he would host. That also proved to be sham: I soon found out that all the questions would have to be submitted in advance on 3 X 5 cards for approval. This man would later decline a request to visit a church member on his deathbed, instead sending a subordinate while he hit the golf course. The dying man's wife related this story to me personally. God spare us from church administrators and give us shepherds!

I briefly attended another church near where we lived out in the country. There the pastor embezzled a $200,000 insurance settlement fund. When I began to ask questions, he called a deacons' meeting and told them I "had a history of causing problems in other churches." Soon he left for Missouri and was never heard from again.

When we left First Baptist Church of Hammond in 1989,

we wound up before long at Fairhaven Baptist Church in Valparaiso, Indiana under Pastor Roger Voegtlin. I have often described Roger Voegtlin as, "Jack Hyles on Steroids minus 50 IQ points." After all these years, I think that in fact, that is a generous assessment, even though he was an outspoken critic of Jack Hyles. The churches ran their buses in many of the same communities as Hyles' buses.

We were in a "New Members Class" at Fairhaven. One day a fellow Hyles-Anderson Seminary graduate approached me and asked me if he could come over to our house with a few people from the class and discuss some concerns that they were having at Fairhaven. I agreed, and before long there were about ten of us gathered in our living room in Lake Station, Indiana. Soon there was a very loud knock at the front door. I opened it to find Roger Voegtlin on our front porch. He had a very, very serious and stern look on his face. He spoke these words to me: "Brother Kaifetz, we heard that you were having a meeting here tonight and the church was going to be discussed. I felt that we ought to be here. We'd like to come in." There was a line of deacons all the way down our driveway to the sidewalk; twenty-two men in all.

Our living room was 400 square feet, so we found room for all of them, although some men were sitting on the floor. My wife immediately left the room and returned less than a minute later to make an announcement. "Somebody is blocking our driveway with their car, and I am leaving. You need to move your car now." The car was a white late model Nissan SUV belonging to Voegtlin. He gave the keys to one of his men with orders to move it.

I told a friend of mine there to go in my office and get my tape recorder and a microphone. He came back with it and I stood up and made an announcement:

"I am going to record this meeting. I know that whatever I say will be deliberately misquoted and otherwise misrepresented to the church, and I am not willing to take that chance. This meeting will be tape recorded."

Voegtlin immediately spoke up and said that he would not go along with that. I answered him very directly:

"Pastor Voegtlin, I am not asking for your permission. This is my house, and I am recording this meeting. If you don't like it, there's the door."

He again would not go along, and so I asked him and the deacons to leave immediately. When he saw that I would not be bullied, he finally relented.

The meeting lasted two-and-a-half hours. Voegtlin would not give an inch: this was his church and his decision to run it like a military boot camp, brass band and all. Toward the end of the meeting, I stood up. I held up a large, maroon Bible and made the following speech: "Gentlemen, this is the Word of God." I then asked them following question: "Can anyone here open this book and show me one teaching in its pages that I have violated?" Heads began to turn downward. Apparently these men thought that this would be a good time to get a good look at the tops of their shoes.

One by one, I went to each man and held my Bible out to them, asking them individually: "Can you show me?" Not one person would answer either "yes" or "no." I went from one man to the next until I stood in front of Roger Voegtlin. I asked him the same question and he said nothing. I then said, "Then it is time for you men to leave my house." They all exited without saying one word. We never went back to Fairhaven Baptist Church, a church where the abuses have reached epic and legendary proportions. (See the Facebook Group, Do Right Fairhaven Baptist Church)

One Sunday in Voegtlin's church not long before this meeting in our home, two teenage girls were talking during the offering. Voegtlin went into a rage and called them out. Then he pointed to their parents a few rows behind us and called them out by name and called them "failures as parents" and told them in front of a packed church that they "should be ashamed to have raised children like these girls!" I remember thinking that this man probably just damaged these girls for life and may well have kept three generations of those families out of church from that day on. All they had done was to whisper during the offering.

I could go on with enough stories like that one to fill several more books. OH COULD I GO ON! That is, however, not the purpose of this book. What I am trying to convey is that the person whose words you have been patiently reading here has a MAJOR LEAGUE bone to pick with the church. In the end, however, I have learned that it is best to do with bones what we do with them in our home: I step out the back door and give them to our 155 pound white German Shepherd, Toby. His animal dining etiquette, canine jaws, sharp incisors, grinding molars and hereditary instincts dispose him far better to deal with a bone than my anatomy and dietary preferences dispose me to gnaw on them. Gnawing on bones is beneath me. I am a child of the King. So are you.

Now let us switch gears for a moment. Let us look at the topic of forgiveness and let us put on our biblical glasses. (Did I say "put on?" Yikes! How about we just never take them off?) I cannot think of the subject of forgiveness without this biblical narrative immediately coming to the forefront of my mind:

"Then came Peter to him, and said, Lord, how oft shall my brother sin against me, and I forgive him? till seven times? Jesus saith unto him, I say not unto thee, Until seven times: but, Until seventy times seven. Therefore is the kingdom of heaven likened unto a certain king, which would take a count of his

servants. And when he had begun to reckon, one was brought unto him, which owed him ten thousand talents. But forasmuch as he had not to pay, his lord commanded him to be sold, and his wife, and children, and all that he had, and payment to be made. The servant therefore fell down, and worshipped him, saying, Lord, have patience with me, and I will pay thee all. Then the lord of that servant was moved with compassion, and loosed him, and forgave him the debt. But the same servant went out, and found one of his fellowservants, which owed him an hundred pence: and he laid hands on him, and took him by the throat, saying, Pay me that thou owest. And his fellowservant fell down at his feet, and besought him, saying, Have patience with me, and I will pay thee all. And he would not: but went and cast him into prison, till he should pay the debt. So when his fellowservants saw what was done, they were very sorry, and came and told unto their lord all that was done. Then his lord, after that he had called him, said unto him, O thou wicked servant, I forgave thee all that debt, because thou desiredst me: Shouldest not thou also have had compassion on thy fellowservant, even as I had pity on thee?"
Matthew 18:21-35

Now does absolutely everything that we need to know and understand about biblical forgiveness come from this passage? No. We have the entire Bible and it is surely within that broader doctrinal context that our understanding should come. Any other method of study relies on "proof texts," and almost always, the position or belief is born first, and the Bible is then used to support it, hammered into a shape that conforms to our "truth." **This is the expression of religious philosophy, not sound Bible preaching.** There has never been a greater or more accomplished master of this method than Jack Hyles. In fact, Hyles himself often told the story of a call he made to John R. Rice, then editor of the Sword of the Lord which published Hyles' sermons regularly. One day Hyles began the conversation with ,"Hello Dr. Rice. Whatcha doing?" Hyles never had any qualms about relating Dr. Rice's immediate response: **"Trying to find some Scripture to go with one of your sermons."** This always elicited much laughter from Hyles' fawning crowds. I wish I could say that it was a nervous laughter, but it sadly was not even that. God, however, was not laughing.

I have been dealing now for three years with an entire church in another state that refuses to forgive. I won't go into any details, because they are not central to our purposes here. (Here is an extensive website dedicated to this church's abusive campaign against their founding pastor: http://www. prospectavenuebaptist.info)

Suffice it to say that I have presented them with many premises and injunctives on God's requirements for forgiveness. I do not necessarily believe that these premises are universal. Here, however, is what I do believe is the position that the Bible indicates on the responsibility for forgiveness directed to Christians:

We are told that we owe others the same brand of forgiveness that Jesus Christ extended to us at the time that we were brought into His fold. So let us then take a look at the dynamic of that forgiveness based on our own personal salvation experience:

• It was undeserved.

• We never implied that it was owed to us.

• We came "without one plea."

• We understood that we had no currency that had any value in that transaction.

150

- We understood what had separated us from God and we came forth with genuine and sincere repentance as a result.

- We had some measure of understanding of the magnitude of Christ's forgiveness and the love that fueled it, thanks to the guidance and instruction of others.

- We understood that we needed to show gratitude, and it began to flow right then and there from our hearts, and the more we learned, the more it flourished.

- We had no desire to minimize, rationalize or justify our sins.

- We understood that we were entering into a new day, a new life, a new standard. WE HAD BEEN BORN AGAIN!

So if someone comes to you now and there seems to be something of the spirit reflected above in their desire to elicit your forgiveness, you have your example on the basis of your response to Jesus as described above. On the other hand, let us say that someone has stolen from you and comes to you and a conversation something like this unfolds:

Thief – "You say you are a Christian, so you need to forgive me."
Victim – I could be willing to forgive you. First you must give me back the money.
Thief – "I don't have it.
Victim – "Where is it."
Thief – "I needed a vacation really badly, so I went on a cruise."
Victim – So are you willing to pay me back the money?"

Thief – "I can't. I lost my job, and besides, you don't need it. You drive a brand new car, you live in a nice house. Why do you need more money?"

Should the victim forgive this person who admits to stealing from him? OF COURSE NOT! There is no repentance and no understanding whatsoever on their part as to the moral shortcomings of their act. They are not sorry. FORGIVING THEM WOULD ONLY MINIMIZE THE SIN! Forgiveness would be an act of enabling. The thief would be empowered because he would feel that he got away with it. One should NEVER, ever extend forgiveness to this kind of person. Simply put, he has not seen his sin as God sees it.

Now the other shoe is going to drop: YOU SHOULD ALWAYS BE MORE THAN WILLING IN YOUR HEART TO FORGIVE SUCH A PERSON WHEN AND IF HE MEETS THE BIBLICAL REQUIREMENTS FOR FORGIVENESS: REPENTANCE AND "GODLY SORROW." That forgiveness should be in your heart and ready to go when the time is right. The love in which that forgiveness is wrapped will insulate you from the bitter acids of resentment, hate and even fear with which an unforgiving heart poisons the bosom in which it beats.

We will not be made whole until you and I can look at the people who imposed untold cultish control and abuse upon us at First Baptist Church of Hammond, or any other controlling cult-like church, and say: **"I am willing from the depths of my heart to forgive you the moment you begin to understand the nature and evil of your church sins, your implied assent to the abuse by your silence, and the offense they presented to a holy and righteous God."** THIS IS HOW JESUS FORGAVE YOU! For you to fail in following His example when forgiveness is not even a consideration for you says but one thing from where I sit: "Yes, Jesus, I know that you forgave me. But this person's sin was so much worse than my sin against You, that I will never forgive." Congratulations: **you have just made yourself God!**

Now a warning, and please believe me when I tell you that I extend it in love, and not in judgment, as it truly does break my heart to see anyone who is hurting from this kind of abuse.

I once sat across from a mother and father at a kitchen table in an old and very sparse concrete house in Gary, Indiana surrounded by a dirt yard and broken toys. Their pre-teen daughter was the molestation victim of A.V. Ballenger, the F.B.C. Hammond church deacon who went to prison for this horrific act done in that very church. I saw that family's pain. I saw their anguish. I saw the father's anger. I saw the aftermath. I cried with them. I sat next to them during Ballenger's three day trial. My wife and I did everything we could for that family for many years. They were devastated not just by what Ballenger had done to their daughter, <u>by the monumental juggernaut of the church that vilified them for daring to speak out against a pedophile deacon</u>.

I also sat on a couch in the front room of a little house in Gary, Indiana and prayed with the mother and father of the eleven year old girl who had been kidnaped by Andy Beith, a former Hyles-Anderson College student, father to Bill Beith. Bill Beith was a Hyles-Anderson College graduate who later made headlines by soliciting a male undercover cop for oral sex in a Northwest Indiana public park.

I was there all day, every day with this family, as TV satellite trucks from Chicago network affiliates lined the street and reporters camped out on their front lawn waiting for any word on their daughter or a glimpse of the family. Finally late one afternoon I said to the father, "Craig, (not his real name) I want to tell you what I believe was an understanding or a thought that I think came from God to me last night.

Jesus is enjoying the fellowship and hours of daily prayer He has known with you since your daughter was taken. He is really delighting in all that time with you. I believe that He will see that your daughter is returned safely, but He loves you so much and so treasures the added time He now spends with you in prayer. He doesn't want to give up the sweetness of all that fellowship with you just yet. I think that if you told Him that it would continue after Samantha (not her real name) is returned, that it could make a difference." I also felt the need to issue a stern warning to my friend: "But PLEASE, Craig, don't tell the Lord that unless you mean it from the depths of your soul."

He answered me right away. "I do mean it, Jerry. Lets pray right now and tell Him." We began to pray, and that prayer was one of the sweetest and most powerful prayers I have ever heard. I am greatly moved years later when I bring it to mind. I am not kidding when I say that just before I opened my tear-filled eyes, I wondered for a brief moment if I would catch a glimpse of Jesus Himself in that room. We felt just that close to Him. It was an indescribable experience.

We got up off the old rattan couch on the enclosed back porch of that tiny house where we had just prayed, and as we walked into the living room, the phone rang. Not more than a minute had passed since our prayer. It was a man named Charlie, the lead F.B.I. agent on the case. Andy Beith, the Christian School principal who had kidnaped the young girl had been on their Ten Most Wanted List. I knew from the father's reaction that this was good news. They had found them, and the daughter was safe and sound and on her way back home from Las Vegas!

There was no containing the joy that erupted in that living room. Even with the doors, windows and curtains all closed, the many reporters out front could not help but realize what had just happened. We were asked by the F.B.I. to not say anything yet, but the media knew.

On a side note, I had gone to Bill Beith, Andy Beith's father, when he was my pastor in Lake Station, Indiana at Liberty Baptist Church. I had brought another church member along. We placed on Pastor Beith's desk a police report from the Gary Police Department detailing a sexual liaison in the back seat of a parked car between his son Andy Beith and a sixteen year old girl from the church. This infuriated this pastor and we were forced out of the church that very week. Andy was now in F.B.I. custody in Las Vegas and would be sentenced to fifteen years in a federal prison.

So you see, I have seen the hurt. I have seen the pain. I have seen the tears. Some of them have been mine. But in all of this over a period of twenty-five years, never have I once been tempted to look unto Jesus and say, "I blame you!" That thought has never crossed my mind. Do I want to vomit when I see an Independent Fundamental Baptist preacher in the pulpit with a thousand times more swagger than humility? Oh, yes, and them some. But the next morning before the sun is up, I will be in my reading chair in my office with an open Bible on my lap and the same prayer on my lips that I have prayed many thousands of times over the decades: *"Lord, open Thou mine eyes that I may behold wondrous things out of thy Law."*

I would like to share as well with you some other thoughts that have been very helpful to me in my Christian life. If this turns out to be a bigger step than you may be willing to take, or a step that is not exactly in a comfortable direction for you, don't worry about it. Come back to it down the road and see how you feel about it. This is just what has worked for me.

It starts with the premise that one of the things that characterizes Jesus Christ is that He suffered unjustly. After all, isn't that really what the cross is all about? I recently reminded a very dear pastor friend of mine, Pastor Dorman Owens, of this. He is now close to eighty and suffering an ENORMOUS injustice, having been left in the ditch of life bloodied and beaten with no Good Samaritan anywhere in sight. There are no words to describe what his church of 38 years did to this man—a group of people most of which were led to the Lord by Pastor Dorman. (see the link on page 150)

I thought to myself that when Jesus really wants us to understand His life on earth, there must be unjust suffering involved. Our earthly mind frames this only in a negative and often tragic light, but I believe that the higher spiritual reality presented is that in fact when we suffer unjustly, we may have been given a wonderful opportunity to live a moment of our life as Jesus lived his entire three years of ministry, culminating in Calvary's cross.

Here are some Bible verses that have helped me to see that in my Christian life:

"Wherefore seeing we also are compassed about with so great a cloud of witnesses, let us lay aside every weight, and the sin which doth so easily beset us, and let us run with patience the race that is set before us, Looking unto Jesus the author and finisher of our faith; who for the joy that was set before him endured the cross, despising the shame, and is set down at the right hand of the throne of God."

"Follow peace with all men, and holiness, without which no man shall see the Lord: Looking diligently lest any man fail of the grace of God; lest any root of bitterness springing up trouble you, and thereby many be defiled;"
Hebrews Chap. 12

Would you care to hear a very down-to-earth synthesis of these verses? Try this one on for size: **DON'T LET THEIR STINK STAY ON YOU!** Wash it off in the cleansing flow of God's grace.

People only stay mired in that kind of stink if they feel powerless. Well, the truth is, YOU ARE ANYTHING BUT POWERLESS! That is one of the reasons why I decided to write this book. It is initially not something that I was well disposed to undertaking, to say the least. However, I had early on, by the grace and mercy of God, found the road to balance, peace, harmony and self-respect when I left First Baptist Church of Hammond in 1990. I believed that I needed to climb the highest tree that I could find and say, "OVER HERE! THIS IS THE WAY OUT!"

I ran down the path at a dead sprint and leaped over the hurdles that others threw in my path like they were pebbles. But please do not think that I am claiming the tiniest bit of credit for this. It ALL comes down to understanding one major principle of the Christian faith. By God's grace and mercy He drilled that into my head early on in my Christian life like it had been shot out of a tank barrel:

> *"So that we may boldly say, The Lord is my helper, and I will not fear what man shall do unto me."*
> Hebrews 13:6

I have been out of church for years at a time. As I understand my Bible, the only command regarding church attendance that is given to Christians is found in Hebrews:

> *"Not forsaking the assembling of ourselves together, as the manner of some is; but exhorting one another: and so much the more, as ye see the day approaching."*
> Hebrews 10:25

I would submit to Christians who have been hurt in church, that this is one of the key verses that we need to understand. The word upon which all of this hinges is the word *"forsaking."* If I am disgusted, or you are bitter and hurt over our similar church experiences, are we right or do we have just cause in just saying, "I am DONE!" and walking away?

In an effort to be honest here, and maybe to give evidence to some that I have no agenda other than to enlighten and help people to heal, I will give you what may be a surprisingly candid answer: <u>I fully understand that sentiment</u>, and I have come very close to expressing it myself on many, many occasions. However, I have to tell you as I would tell a close friend or brother or sister or son or daughter, I really don't think that is the pathway to peace or the avenue of God's blessing in your life. There is life, there is hope, there is joy, there is Christian growth outside of the Independent Fundamental Baptist Movement, just as there is hope within it for those who will seek God with a pure heart and with a proper understanding of pastoral authority in a healthy and well balanced church.

When people ask me if I am a Fundamentalist, I always give the same answer: "<u>I believe the fundamentals of the Christian faith</u>." I can often tell by the look on their face that what they really meant was, **"Do you belong to my club?"** If they had asked that question more honestly and phrased it that way, they would have gotten a one word answer: "NO!"

What I am saying is, **be true to the principles of Jesus Christ**. Stay in the Bible, and understand why God put Hebrews 10:25 in the Bible: don't ever give up permanently on finding a good church. YES, I understand and thoroughly respect anyone deciding that "there ain't no such animal" as a "good church" out there. I understand.

Against what seemed to be slimmer and slimmer odds that there was a good church out there I somehow held out hope and had faith for twenty-two years after leaving First Baptist Church of Hammond. By the grace of God, I am now in a good church. Is it perfect? No. Does it have the word "Baptist" in it's name? Yes. Would I like to see more expository preaching there? Yes. Am I disappointed that the church often seems quite content in their "comfort zone?" Are there some folks there whose understanding of biblical Christianity is occasionally disappointing? Yes, as mine undoubtedly daily is to God.

Yes, the Scriptures do talk about the relationship of a Christian to church. The word "forsaking" in Hebrews is the Greek word "*kataleipo*." It means. "To leave behind." Another definition from the Greek lexicon is" to leave to a person or thing by ceasing to care for it." Interestingly, it is often applied to the dying. Dying people are no fun to be around. It is after a depressing and sad time, but you can bet that if they are one of His, that Jesus is there with them. It doesn't matter sometimes as you sit beside someone's deathbed if they were a contributor to their own demise. At that moment, what matters most is not whether they hurt you or took advantage of you. At the very least, give them the benefit of your prayer from a heart willing to forgive, like the heart Jesus has for you. That will be when you know that you are healed.

"For whatsoever is born of God overcometh
the world: and this is the victory that overcometh
the world, even our faith."
1 John 5:4

"When the Pope speaks 'ex-cathedra,' Catholics believe that it is God speaking. I saw that same mentality at First Baptist Church of Hammond."

Chapter

17

Renewed Vigilance

I grew up in two cultures: America and France. What any American first notices in visiting a country like France, is that it is a very old country. In traveling through France with my family as a young boy, I still remember seeing Roman ruins in many places we visited. I remember Roman aqueducts, Roman arches and Roman fountains in villages. I always wanted to touch these monuments, because when I did, I felt connected to history.

One of the places I visited was Carcassonne. Carcassonne is a fortified French town in the the Provence region of Southern France. First fortified by the Romans around 100 BC, this town became the most fortified city in the world. It has been fully restored and today is the most magnificent example of a fortified city anywhere. You can only imagine the impression this town made on me when I gazed up from the "Ville Basse" (lower city) as a six year old boy and saw the massive fortified walls that seemed to tower to the sky and to go on forever.

In the days of the Visigoths, the Gauls (related to the Galatians), and the Romans, there were plenty of reasons to live behind fortified walls. The history of these medieval fiefdoms is the history of conquest and conflict. The walls of Carcassonne today stand as a monument to the existential threats of human existence. They testify as to who man is.

If there is anything inherent in what I consider to be a well founded Christian world view, it is to be found in a statement Jesus once made that has been inexpressibly undervalued by Christians for two thousand years:

"*...He knew what was in man.*"
John 2:25

We could visit a seminary and sit in on a 700 level class on Systematic Theology and tune in on a discussion of the doctrine of The Total Depravity of Man. Or we could just go sit under a tree somewhere and clear our minds and reflect on these six words of Jesus. Having done both, I would recommend the later.

So was Jesus a cynic? Was He just bitter and negative? Was He a pessimist? Did He not see any redeeming value in man? Well, this is where we have to be exceedingly careful. Like so many things that Jesus said, if we just run by them in the sprint of life and grab a handful of meaning, briefly examine our prize and stuff it in our pocket, we will miss a lot. In fact, we will often in our haste or carelessness miss our pocket and gain nothing. Such is the case with the verse above.

If we will look at what Jesus said, we will see that, yes, He knew *"what was in man,"* but He did not suggest that it was ALL that was in man! Was Jesus perhaps saying that man, though never to be fully trusted, had an innate capacity for good? Under the right circumstances, under the right influence, under the right guidance, under the right teaching, and in the right environment, is man not capable of a nobility of character and a largesse of heart and soul that can bless an individual or a generation? Jesus was only saying that He knew that man was prone to imperfection and so his life required moral structure, nurturing, and example. This is why He invented the New Testament Church.

So what does this have to do with a six year old kid visiting Carcassonne? Plenty! Because once you build these kinds of people and create a stabilizing Christian environment in which they can live, YOU HAD BETTER BUILD A WALL AROUND IT! Once the travail of an honest and sincere pastor has moved people in the church closer to the goal expressed by the Apostle Paul of *"Christ formed in you,"* there comes a duty to protect. Just ask Nehemiah when he was building his wall and Sanballat, and Tobiah, and Geshem did everything they could to get him to stop. Nehemiah's answer to them has resounded down through the ages as one of the most inspirational and exemplary responses to those who would ridicule God's people in their efforts to separate themselves from what, like Jesus, they knew to be in man:

"I am doing a great work, so that I cannot come down: why should the work cease, whilst I leave it, and come down to you?"
Nehemiah 6:3

"Should such a man as I flee?" asked Nehemiah. Nehemiah wasn't proud; he just knew whom he represented and the inherent nobility of what he had set out to do. Then when it was all done, Nehemiah speaks three words. These three words symbolize the very reason the wall was built. They express what the people are now to do inside those walls. These three words chart a course. They connect the lives of the wall builders to the wall Designer. They are three of the most important words in all the Bible. They are words that we should repeat in our homes every day, and in our churches every time we gather. Once the wall is built, Nehemiah directs these words to Ezra the Scribe"

"BRING THE BOOK!"
Nehemiah 8:1

What transpired then is to many inspirational. To others it brings reassurance. To some it brings hope. For me, my reaction comes in one word: predictable. Ezra stood "on a pulpit of wood", surrounded by 13 good men (Mattithiah, Shema, Anaiah, Urijah, Hilkiah, Maaseiah, Pedaiah, Mishael, Malchiah, Hashum, Hashbadana, Zechariah, and Meshullam), and he read the book.

> *"...and the ears of all the people were attentive unto the book of the law."*
> Nehemiah 8:3

Not only that, but the preaching was **EXPOSITORY** (verse by verse), and thirteen other men along with the Levites began to exegete and bring out the meaning of what Ezra had read for the people to help them to better understand. Of that the Bible account leaves no doubt:

> *"So they read in the book in the law of God distinctly, and gave the sense, and caused them to understand the reading."*
> Nehemiah 8:3

THANK GOD FOR EXPOSITORY PREACHING!

Building that wall without having the purpose that Nehemiah had, and the capacity for leadership that he displayed would have been an exercise in sheer vanity, if not utter futility. Finally, in the end, the mockery of his boisterous critics notwithstanding, the wall was built. Then they gathered a "CALLED OUT ASSEMBLY." Call this what you will, I call that a CHURCH! That kind of church is the reason for the wall!

In my few brief decades as a Christian, I have seen what I can only describe as the influx of Catholic thinking in the Independent Fundamental Baptist Movement. The Catholic Church was largely founded on the basis on Augustine's theology. Augustine taught that the bishops and priests of

164

the Church are the successors of the Apostles and that their authority in the Church is God given. This is why the Roman Catholic Church has had a history of conflict with civil government. Those governments saw the authority of the church as a threat, and rightly so. The Catholic Church claims legitimacy for its bishops and priests via the doctrine of apostolic succession and the authority of the Pope via the supposedly unbroken line of popes, claimed as successors to Simon Peter. When he speaks "ex cathedra" (from the chair), Catholics believe that it is God speaking. Make no mistake, I saw the same mentality at First Baptist Church of Hammond.

As the church became more of a hierarchical institution, the bishop emerged as an increasingly authoritative figure. Before long, his influence turned to responsibility for a realm well beyond the local church concept illustrated in the Book of Acts. In time, the Bishop of Rome came to be considered "first among equals." The church was becoming increasingly centralized. <u>Centralization of power has always been the enemy of the Christian</u> liberty owed to every believer-priest and paid for with the blood of Jesus Christ. With Constantine's conversion to Christianity in 313, the Bishop of Rome received new prestige, which he used to grow his influence and authority even more until today, it is worldwide.

This is the pattern that I have seen in the Independent Fundamental Baptist Movement. We jokingly once referred to Jack Hyles as the "Baptist Pope." People got a chuckle out of that, but I understand now that God wasn't laughing. These doings in the first three centuries of the church centralized power to the point where the Inquisition was possible, lasting for several centuries and resulting in the deaths by torture of many millions of "unrepentant heretics."

Today, the local church is in many ways no longer local. Unlike Southern Baptists who are a part of the Southern Baptist Convention, Independent Baptists would reject the notion that they are part of a denomination. I would completely disagree. I have been to too many I.F.B. mass meetings presided over by our very own "Bishop of Rome" with Augustine's "City of God" book figuratively tucked under his arm. I watched Jack Hyles as he called up one I.F.B. hero after another to the pulpit of First Baptist Church of Hammond. Like the Apostle Paul,"... ***they who seemed to be somewhat in conference added nothing to me."*** (Galatians 2:6)

Not long ago in a church service that I attended, just such a gathering took place. A member of that church came up to me looking around at all the guest preachers and said, "Man, I don't know if I have ever been in one room where there has been this kind of power." I was angered and disgusted by this statement. I felt like saying to this fellow, "How about we stick with Jesus as our hero? I hear He isn't real big on sharing His glory with others." Not all that many years ago, I would have said much worse to him. What I did say to this man was simply,"Oh, I don't know that there isn't some little old lady in a back pew somewhere that isn't closer to God than the whole lot of these guys put together." He chuckled and said, "Yeah, you might be right, brother." I had no doubt that I was. (One of these men was a preacher whom I had warned about Jack Schaap a year before Schaap's demise. Despite the corroborated details I shared wit him, he continued in his support of Schaap. This story is in the appendix.)

So how do we maintain independence in our churches? Do we want to add the words, "Hermetically Sealed" to our church signs? Do we, like the Jehovah's Witnesses, want buildings with no windows, figuratively or literally? How do we protect our churches from the many infections, diseases, poisons and viruses in the religious world? Do we make our churches walled cities like Carcassonne? Do we tell evangelists that they are no longer welcome because of the ecclesiastical or doctrinal viruses they may carry from their travels? Do we stop sending our young people to Bible colleges and seminaries?

My first suggestion is that churches, pastors and Christians all pull their heads out of the sand. This is a new world we live in today and one of the main reasons for that can be expressed in two words: <u>SOCIAL MEDIA</u>. Yes, the Internet is a vast wasteland, but so is television; so what do you say to someone who came to Christ watching a Billy Graham Crusade on TV? Should he have thrown out his TV, as some I.F.B. preachers have suggested? Does the Social Media have a role to play in evangelism today? Are Baptists going to once again reach for their Amish hats?

Sadly, the downside of Conservatism is that we are so often the last to catch on to the great benefits of the new tools and technologies. Practically speaking, we wear our Amish hats to discussions about the cutting edge communications tools of today, if we even show up at all. Some show up just to deride anyone suggesting Independent Baptists think outside the proverbial box. There are lost souls outside that box. I know of a very well known pastor who has pastored a large and successful church. He has been looked up to in the Independent Fundamental Movement for many years. I have always enjoyed hearing him preach and I think his doctrine is sound and I have no reason to not believe that he lives a moral life. I know of nothing bad about him personally that has ever been said. However, if he came to my church to preach next Sunday, I would walk out. Why? I recently learned that he had preached at First Baptist Church of Hammond in 2011 and Hyles Anderson College in September of 2012.

So am I saying that he is guilty by association? YES! YES! YES! and <u>A THOUSAND TIMES YES</u>! I would say to this brother: the handwriting on moral corruption in the Independent Fundamental Baptist Movement has not been on the wall; IT HAS BEEN PUBLISHED FROM COAST TO

COAST FOR TWENTY-FIVE YEARS! So if you choose to stand in that pulpit under the sponsorship of those corrupt, depraved and vile men, then <u>YOU BRING THAT STENCH TO MY CHURCH</u> when you come to speak! Yes, I will walk out!

To preach under the sponsorship of a corrupt institution is to legitimize that institution. Sadly, the effect can only be to corrupt and compromise you when you make the choice to sit in those pews and listen, or to allow those men in your church pulpit.

THAT is the influence from which I believe every church needs to protect itself. Do we quit inviting speakers or evangelists? No, but how about we work a little harder to train some of our own? How about we ask the great-grandmas and grandpas in the back rows to stand up and tell the folks how good Jesus has been to them in their lives? I don't know about you, but for me as a preacher, those are often tough acts to follow! Those testimonies MOVE people! I have only been in two genuine revivals where the Holy Spirit came through a church like a freight train, and both times they started in the pews, not the pulpit. Both times they were started by women testifying.

If a church decides to send its young people off to a Christian college, I have but one piece of advice: <u>DO YOUR HOMEWORK</u>! You OWE your young people that! Appoint a committee of discerning folks to spend a month researching schools. And for the love of God, DON'T BYPASS THE SOCIAL MEDIA! Find the local newspapers online and search out anything about the school. Be responsible parents. Be responsible grandparents. Be responsible Youth Pastors. I am not suggesting that you look for the perfect school, any more than I think you are likely to find the perfect church, but you should have a standard of conduct and reputation below which you will not acquiesce in entrusting your children to people you have never met. That is of course no substitute for instilling in them wisdom, discernment and a dedication to righteousness. It is more like being responsible enough to find a safe park for them to run in, not a vacant lot strewn with broken glass and bullet casings.

I have been blessed in my post-I.F.B. days. My wife and I have found a good church. I think by now, you know that the last word in the English lexicon that would describe me is the word naïve. If someone wants to think that I am naïve in thinking that I am in a good church, I would not engage that person in any way. Have at it. What I do understand is that I have not found a perfect church. There are a couple of folks there that absolutely and unquestionably rub me the wrong way. I am content to give them leeway. Is there as much expository preaching there as I would like to see? No. However, when we joined that church a year ago, my personal healing reached a higher level. The interesting thing is, I didn't know I was sick.

I had never been inclined to count myself among the I.F.B. Movement's "walking wounded." I knew that I had dished it out for years far more than I had taken anything from anyone in that crowd. Yet after a number of years of being out of church, I had lost something very valuable. I consider myself a fairly good writer, but I don't know that I can put my finger on what was missing in my life . . . . in my heart . . . . in my soul. I just knew that now it was coming back. That is why I look forward to going to church for the first time in so many, many years. It is a good feeling that I never expected to have. If I can get there, you can find your way there also.

I read the letters that have been coming my way every week since this book was announced. Are these to me just the narratives of one more account of abuse when I read them? Oh, no! They hit me right in the gut every time. Some tear my heart out. Some bring tears. Others make me want to get my gun.

I would repeat here what I have said earlier in this book: if you have been victimized by these vile men and their corrupt institutions and you come to the place where you never want to see the inside of a church again, I am one who understands. In fact, if it were not for my providential landing in the church that we are in now, I too would find something else to do with my Sundays for the foreseeable future beside going to church, and maybe for the rest of my life.

We moved a thousand miles to be in our church. In the Summer of 2011, we sold our home in Northwest Indiana, along with ninety percent of what we owned. This was the land of spiritual corruption for me. What pastors were not morally corrupt were self-serving rascals for whom I had lost respect, except for one, Pastor Bruce Ison. There seemed to be no end to them. It was time to leave, or to allow those men in church pulpit.

A good friend of mine of 40 years asked me if when we got to the end of our long driveway in late August of 2011, if I looked back on our 5,000 square foot home that we had built ourselves, our picturesque private lake, our ponds, the timber bridge, the waterfall, the orchard, the big fountain, the sand beach, the big red barn, the thousands of Pines we planted, the buildings, the sawmill, the happy times fishing, swimming, kayaking, picking wildflowers, watching the deer and foxes and waterfowl, and if I had any regrets about leaving. I didn't have to think about my answer for one second: "NO REGRETS!" It was just time to go. Any landscape without a good church is a barren place.

After the move, we joined the church the first Sunday we attended. We had been visiting there on our trips to Texas for several years. My wife's jaw dropped when I told her that was the plan. People who knew me thought I was either kidding or had taken leave of my senses. I understood these reactions completely.

But what about you? Is there a church for you? You think I am going to say "yes," don't you? Sorry, but one of my goals in writing this book was to be honest. The best answer to that question that I can give you is, "maybe." Most churches that I have known that are not outright compromised are at best promoters of the status-quo and nothing more. They are comfortable where they are and they have every intention of staying that way. The preacher is there to deliver "three points and a poem" and preserve his pension.

There is no office that I respect any more highly than the office of pastor in the New Testament Church. That being said, there is no group of men for whom I have had more disdain in the last twenty-five years than pastors. If you are reading this book for the same reason that most readers probably are, that statement requires to further explanation. But how can anyone reconcile that statement with others that I have made in these pages about the pastors whom I have admired and so greatly respected? There have been three in thirty years.

I'm not sure how to explain the reconciliation of those two seemingly divergent perspectives. All I can tell you is that when you find such a man, you'll know it. What I can tell you without question is this: there is one principal characteristic that must be in place in such a man. If you don't see it from day one, WALK AWAY! No wait . . . don't walk . . . . RUN!!!

So what is it? What is it that is as beautiful and inspiring as the "Fundamentalist swagger" is disgusting? What is it that men like Jack Hyles and Jack Schaap lacked the most? What is the last word that comes to mind in describing these villains of the pulpit? What is it that eventually made me realize, "This man does not know Jesus." What should you be looking for in a man who dares to step in the pulpit every Sunday and claim to represent Jesus Christ? I can tell you in one word:

<u>Humility</u>!

"...for God resisteth the proud,
and giveth grace to the humble."
I Peter 5:5

Chapter

18

The Missing Element In Fundamentalism

Born around 1915 B.C., Joseph was the older son of Rachel and a favorite with his father Jacob. Reuben, the firstborn, never achieved the status or love in his father's eyes that traditionally should have been his, instead seeing this privilege extended to his younger brother, Joseph. Jacob's love for his son Joseph is evidenced by the royal tunics he made for Joseph. These were characterized by long, flowing sleeves, distinguishing him to his brothers as the object of a special love by his father, a favored status that meant everything in a patriarchal culture. The "many colors" were probably additional pieces, perhaps sleeves, making the garment even more special due to the costly nature of fabric dyes and their special significance.

These gifts tell us that Joseph's elevated position in his father's eyes was so significant that Joseph was scarcely expected to do any menial work. Joseph had a very special relationship with his father, Jacob. Jacob has always been one of my great heroes because he was not willing to take "no" for an answer when it came to having God's blessing on his life. A man of extraordinary wisdom, Jacobhad expressed many years before, his understanding of the necessity of God's blessing upon his life. *"I will not let thee go except thou bless me,"* he had told the Angel of God after a night of wrestling. The blessing was given. There at the ford of Jabok, where two streams meet as they flowed east into Jordan between the Sea of Galilee and the Dead Sea, Jacob received his new name, Israel, "a prince with God." Jacob knew what it was to have special relationship with one's father.

In this same way as Jacob bestowed a special position upon Joseph, Jacob would later choose Ephraim as "first-born" instead of Joseph's oldest son Manasseh (Gen. 48:8-20.) This practice was not uncommon in the patriarchal age, but became forbidden under future Israelite law (Deut. 21:15-17). A generation earlier, Isaac's second son, Jacob was chosen by God to inherit the promises He had made to Isaac. God conveyed the supreme blessing on the family of Jacob: they would be the lineage leading to the Messiah. What a seemingly unlikely choice this was.

Jacob had developed anything but an enviable reputation while growing up. He had tricked his brother Esau and lied to his father so that he could steal Esau's birthright. He then fled to his uncle Laban's home, there getting a painful and trying dose of his own medicine of deception and trickery. Nevertheless, God saw past all that and kept faith in Jacob's underlying qualities of character, giving him a good wife and great possessions. Upon returning to his homeland in Palestine, he found that God had prepared the way for him, as Jacob was restored in fellowship to his brother Esau. There was something about Jacob that God surely liked.

One day Joseph found himself shackled in a slave caravan on his way to what then promised to be a life of complete servitude in the land of Egypt. Joseph's father Jacob, the master of deception in his youth, had now himself been cruelly deceived. Joseph's fate had come at the hands of Jacob's boys. They brought back to their father Joseph's tunic dipped in sheep blood. "I will go down to Sheol mourning for my son," Jacob cried out when he was handed the tunic. The half-existence of the place of the departed seemed no worse than the agony Jacob knew he would face for the rest of his life, having lost the most precious treasure of his later years.

This period was undoubtedly the low point of Joseph's life. Joseph had gone from a life of privilege and a home filled with his father's love and admiration, to being evaluated for servitude by having his teeth examined in a manner befitting a beast of burden. It certainly did not take him long to understand that such was to be his lot in a land he had only heard about, and that probably in anything but favorable terms.

As his brothers turned for Hebron, Joseph saw his sole link with the only world he had ever known vanish out of his sight. His expectations for his life had been distorted like the waving heat rising from those burning desert sands. He had gone from a life of honor, privilege and affection to the lowest rung of the cultural ladder in the ancient middle east: he was a slave! Can we imagine the depth of sorrow and grief that Joseph must have felt that sweltering afternoon in an arid desert? This was a separation that appeared as nothing short of life-long for Joseph. He had no hope of ever seeing his father Jacob or his mother Rachel again. He must have felt abandoned, isolated and completely alone on that dusty road.

In fact, Joseph was not alone. Each step that he took, though indescribably agonizing and heartbreaking to Joseph, was a step ordained by the very Creator of the universe. God had a plan for Joseph. He had a purpose so vast and important in mind, that there probably was not a solitary figure anywhere in the world at that moment that so embodied the unlikelihood of being cast in a role such as God had ordained for Joseph. Joseph was not at all alone on that desert trade-route. Neither was he without the essential elements of his destiny firmly in his possession—he had his character, his faith and he had a close and abiding relationship with his God.

On the other hand, Joseph was only human. As surely as the soul is prone to thoughts of desperation in trying times, Joseph must have been in the abject depths of despondence during that journey south into Egypt.

God's reaction to Joseph's plight, however, was anything but despondent. Just as the Bible tells us that it "pleased God" to see His Son sacrificed on the cross, so must God also have been pleased as He gazed down on a young man whose life had just been torn from its roots. God knew the magnificent future of Joseph's redemptive role in Israel's history. Surely God's response was not anything like Joseph's. While Joseph saw nothing but the shackles on his feet and the back of the slave before him, God saw beyond the horizon of Joseph's despair. Joseph's heart and soul must have cried out with every step: "Why? Why? Why? God, please help me! Take me home!" We can easily guess God's calming and reassuring answer, needing only three words to be expressed: "Trust me, Joseph." And trust Him Joseph did.

Joseph later became a servant in the household of Potiphar. Joseph's previous knowledge of tending flocks and his honest character were not lost on Potiphar. Egyptians were extremely concerned with fraud and theft by laborers. Later, as Potiphar no doubt found Joseph trustworthy and able, the young man was appointed steward over Potiphar's personal residence. It is recorded that *"his master saw that the Lord was with him"* (Gen. 39:2). Joseph continued in his personal relationship with God. It was all he had in Egypt, but it was all he needed.

Joseph was doubtless an exceptionally attractive young man. His mother Rachel *"was beautiful and well favored"* (Gen: 29:17). Joseph's beauty, inside and out, was not lost on Potiphar's wife.

After observing Joseph daily going about his duties in their house, she brazenly makes an open proposition to Joseph: "Lie with me." Virtue is attractive even to the morally bankrupt.

Joseph's life was thrown into turmoil at this very thought. First he tries to explain to the woman that this would be a betrayal of the trust her husband had placed in him. Joseph tries to reason with her and fails. Seeing that his efforts were falling on deaf ears, Joseph reaches farther within himself and brings out the core reason preventing him from committing adultery with the woman

"How then can I do this great wickedness
and sin against God?"
(Gen. 39:9)

Here we have the very display of the greatest and most magnificent of all biblical anchors to steady the human soul in the face of temptation: **SIN DEFINED AS AN OPEN BETRAYAL OF GOD'S PERSONAL TRUST IN THE BELIEVER!** This is where the believer's relationship is elevated above ritual, above tradition, above formal worship and the systematic, stylized approach of religion. This is where true religion rises above a codified set of rules or mere patterns for behavior. Here Joseph makes a statement whose importance it is impossible to overestimate: **OUR ULTIMATE REFUSAL TO ENGAGE IN THE COMPROMISE OF SIN IS ONLY AS STRONG AS OUR PERSONAL RELATIONSHIP WITH OUR GOD** and our refusal to sacrifice that closeness for the pleasures of the world. Joseph's refusal to sin with his master's wife led to her false accusations and to a dark jail cell for Joseph.

God's close relationship with Joseph continued in his imprisonment. ***"God was with Joseph"*** we are told ***"and showed him mercy"*** (Gen. 39:21) Joseph had something inside that royal prison that proved to be far more valuable than all the possessions of those outside the prison, regardless of their quantity or worldly value. He had a personal relationship with his God, and he had learned to trust God in the darkest of times. Make no mistake, these were dark times for Joseph. They are recorded in the beautiful and wrenching poetry of Psalms describing Joseph's torture.

> *"He sent a man before them, even Joseph,*
> *who was sold for a servant:*
> *Whose feet they hurt with fetters:*
> *he was laid in iron:"*
> Psalm 105

Over time, even in prison, the radiance of God's presence about Joseph shone as it always had. Joseph was soon elevated to a supervisory position over the other prisoners. For two more years, he wondered if he would ever be set free. Surely he thought of the injustices that had been his lot—not only the one that had landed him in prison, but the one that had torn him from his family at the hands of his merciless and evil brothers.

If ever there was a mortal soul justified in drawing the human conclusion that life was unfair, it is hard to bring to mind anyone more justified in that point of view than Joseph. Somehow, Joseph did not abandon his faith in the mercy and justice of God. Somehow, Joseph kept in the back of his mind the seldom considered fact that God has all of eternity to make up for the injustices wrought by a cruel world in the lives of His children. Joseph had no Bible, no church, no pastor, no fellow-believers, no songbook, and there is no record of Joseph having even one person to express care and concern for him as a human being in the midst of these prison trials involving even the torture described for us in the Psalm above. Yet with all that, Joseph was able to draw on what he had learned from Rachel and Jacob, his parents. He gloriously succeeded in sustaining his spirits THROUGH HIS RELATIONSHIP WITH GOD. Even in the dark recesses of a federal dungeon in a far away land, with the crushing weight of an unjust accusation leveled at him because of his refusal to betray the trust and love of God, Joseph trusted his God.

It is difficult for some even today to understand the nature and the level of this kind of inner victory in a human being. Few of us posses the ability to completely base our life, our actions and our outlook on the reality of a spiritual world that we cannot see. We live and relate rather on the physical circumstances that daily oppress us and weigh so heavily on our souls. Joseph, like Paul and Silas who two millennia later would sing songs of faith while shackled in another prison,magnificently demonstrated in Pharaoh's prison what it means to have a meaningful relationship with God. This Joseph does under the kind of circumstances that would have caused many to conclude that God had abandoned them to the whim and cruelty of an uncaring world and an abusive system. What a testimony of strength and hope is this man, Joseph!

Joseph's words to Pharaoh in a later meeting with the Egyptian sovereign bear strong and eloquent testimony that his faith had not been damaged by his ordeal: ***"God shall give Pharaoh an answer of peace."*** Joseph gave Pharaoh advice that had been tried and tested in a desert pit and in a dungeon: God is your living resource!

The same closeness to God that had comforted and protected Joseph from false accusations would continue to be his strength. That divine closeness had sheltered him from the harshness of prison life, from the collapse of his faith, and

179

from giving in to the walls of despair seeking daily to close in on him from all sides. That close walk with his God would now protect Joseph from equally ominous risks: self-exaltation and pride, and personal familiarity with the heathen beliefs and practices that would become a part of his own immediate family in Egypt. Joseph never lost sight of the fact that he was "a stranger and a pilgrim" in Egypt. The magnificence of his palace, the adulations and honors of a bowing populace, the praise of a royal Pharaoh could not impose upon Joseph the temptation to turn from the faith of his father Jacob, his grandfather Isaac, and his great-grandfather Abraham.

Joseph later gave his sons Hebrew, not Egyptian names. His heart did not belong to Egypt, it belonged to his father's homeland, rested in his father's promises, awaited return to his father's ancestral home, and most important of all, **HIS HEART BELONGED TO THE GOD OF ABRAHAM, ISAAC AND JACOB!** Joseph knew who he was, and the most formidable of the world's empires, the most ignominious of injustices could not convince him otherwise, whether the trial of faith came to him in a prison cell or upon a gilded throne.

Joseph's close walk with God also accomplished another miracle: it kept the bitterness toward his own brothers who had savagely betrayed him from poisoning his heart. One day, those brothers came calling in Egypt after a famine had come to their own land. Joseph, as we all know, initially concealed his identity from them. Finally, it is all too much for Joseph to bear. The heart that had sustained betrayal, imprisonment, injustice and despair could contain itself no longer. His ability to restrain his emotions had reached its limit. His passions overwhelm him. No longer can he keep his true identity a secret he shouts out: "I AM JOSEPH!" A surge of tears, joy, relief and an outpouring of sentiments too powerful for him to contain for another second exploded from Joseph's heart. The literal translation of the text is, **"he** *gave forth his voice in weeping."*

Joseph's brothers are speechless. They are undoubtedly struck with the paralyzing fear that the most evil and heinous act of their lives now stands personified before them with the power to not only confront them, but to demand the accountability that they surely know is now theirs to pay. But Joseph moves immediately to reassure them: *"God did send me before you to preserve life,"* he declares, compassionately expressing the forgiving nature of God by lifting from their shoulders the immense and unbearable guilt of their sins. What a glorious forward looking glimpse of Christ this is!

Joseph seeks even to place those motives which were designed to destroy his life under the sovereign and gracious providence of God's purposeful and loving plan. No wonder Joseph stands out in the Old Testament as a type of Christ without equal in the eyes of so many! Who today can deny Joseph's betrayals, his elevation to royal stature, his depth of love for his father, his messianic role in saving his people, or their ultimate submission before him in repentance of their sins?

Of all the Bible stories that will be eternally relived, witnessed and enjoyed by the blessed heavenly population sitting before the throne of God, it is doubtful that any will exude the fragrance of a sweeter spirit, a stronger faith, of a more steadfast refusal to abandon one's belief in the innate goodness of God than will the life of Joseph. His faith and courage not only blessed nations, but brought together empires and preserved the lineage to the Messiah Himself. That is what a human being can accomplish when they live the life they are given within a close and personal relationship with God.

God had transformed the evil of a group of Joseph's brothers into a great work of epic and historical redemption.

Joseph not only saved the future lives of three million people in Egypt, but more importantly, <u>he testified to the power and mercy of a great and living God who works personally in the lives of all those who will look to Him in the most disparaging and hopeless of circumstances</u>. God works His goodness even through the evil plans of wicked men. Amenemhet III (1841–1792 B.C.) was the reigning Pharaoh at the time of Joseph's death. Today, we name our dogs Pharaoh, but we name our sons Joseph!

God blessed Joseph with a long life of 110 years. On his deathbed, Joseph reaffirmed his lifelong faith in the promises of God. He reassured those whom he was leaving behind that God would continue to bless their family. In His time, God would keep His promise to Abraham to give Canaan to his descendants (Gen. 12:7; 26:3; 35:12; 46:4). The phrase, "Abraham, Isaac and Jacob" became the standard way of referring to God's covenant with the nation of Israel. The recital of the three names reaffirms the reliability of God's promise and His commitment to fulfill it through an earthly relationship with the heirs of that promise.

Joseph's last act, it may rightfully be said, was to disown Egypt and to firmly identify himself with the budding nation of Israel. Joseph chose near poverty, contempt and the lot of the wayfaring shepherds over the riches and splendor of the Egyptian empire. In this great act of faith, Joseph shows that in his heart, he is true to his God to the end. Of this he leaves no doubt as he speaks his last words: ***<u>I die and God will surely visit you, and bring you out of this land unto the land which He sware to Abraham, Isaac and Jacob.</u>***" His last deed was to require of his descendants to take a solemn oath to insure that even his bones will not be left behind at the time of the Exodus. He made it abundantly clear that his heart had never left the land of his birth, and that his very bones should be returned to the sacred land of his forefathers. Joseph trusted God to the end.

Joseph died and his body was mummified and laid in an Egyptian coffin made of Sycamore wood carved in the general outline of the body. Even in his death, Joseph was speaking to his descendants, telling them that they were never to consider Egypt their home, but to always look toward their return to the land of God's promise to their ancestors. Over four centuries of silence from God were to follow. God apparently believed that Joseph's testimony, based on three previous generations of divine promises, was sufficient. The torch of divine promise, heroic faith, inspiring unimaginable courage would have to cast its light through this long period of suffering in the midst of idolatry until God raised up another deliverer for His people. That man's name was Moses.

Joseph's life is a century long and eloquent statement lived out before the world: <u>THE ABILITY OF GOD TO ACHIEVE JUSTICE IN ONE'S LIFE IS NOT LIMITED BY THE DISCOURAGING OR OPPRESSIVE NATURE OF THE CIRCUMSTANCES OR INSTITUTIONS THAT SURROUND OR DOMINATE US</u>!

Joseph was able to maintain a calmness within that bore a testimony to his faith—a faith so powerful that throughout his life, those who were completely ignorant of its divine source were compelled to recognize its presence in the life and soul of Joseph, and to gaze upon it in admiration.

Joseph's faith in the goodness of God was so real that there seemed to be quite literally nothing that could shake it from him. When he found himself in a pit in the desert, a tortuous and unbearable place by any standard, he knew that he was not alone. When he was drawn from that pit only to be shackled as a human beast of burden and separated from all that he had known his entire life, he refused to be consumed by either grief or bitterness toward his betrayers or his captors.

Joseph's life bears strong and convincing testimony that the most precious resource a human being can have, his faith in God, need never be within the grasp of even the most tortuous circumstances or the most unscrupulous and evil of perpetrators.

Joseph's life was an ongoing expression of the reality that God uses even the most dreadful experiences to shape our lives. One of the most powerful truths gloriously exhibited in Joseph's life is that <u>GOD TAKES EVEN THE EXPERIENCES IN OUR LIVES FROM WHICH THERE IS NO SEEMING WAY OUT, AND CHISELS FROM THEM ASTOUNDING VICTORIES</u>! Yes, the chisel often hurts. Yes, we often fail to see God's hand wrapped around the hurtful grip of the oppressor on that chisel. In the end, however, the stately magnificence of God's glorious outcome can make even the most tortured of souls raise a triumphant voice of testimony to the rest of us myopic and battered souls and echo the words of another tortured soul, David:*"It is good for me that I have been afflicted, that I might learn thy statutes."* (Psalm 119:71) Few ever reach that lofty peak, but we can gaze out at it in the distance and imagine the view from that summit. Can we climb it as did David and Joseph? Oh yes! Yes, we can!

It did not matter for Joseph how dismal were the circumstances. God used those circumstances as building blocks for a brand-new life. Who would believe for a moment that when Joseph was on his way to Egypt as a nameless face in a slave trader's caravan that he could have thought to himself: "I know what I'll do. I'll get into the household of a rich family and I'll work my way up and some day I'll be the Prime Minister and have power and wealth and fame!" Such thoughts were light years from seeming possible under those circumstances in the mind of any rational human being.

All over the world, people live their entire lives in a vain effort to structure the circumstances of their lives. Their goal is to bring them fleeting moments of pleasure or inner peace. For the majority, this entails dulling the senses in some fashion to limit the perception of the reality around them that would remind them that the circumstances surrounding them prevent their being genuinely happy. For those who trust in God, however, the precious nature of this relationship is such an awe-inspiring thing in and of itself, that the glow of its reality melts away the trifling influence of outward circumstances. Joseph lived his entire life in this manner. In doing so he passed tests that would have surely buckled our knees and for many, left our hearts broken for life, and our faith in ruin. **JOSEPH KEPT HIS EYES FIXED ON GOD**, and his pain, his tragedies, and the evil things that were done to him were used by God to make something enduring and legendary out of his life that so brilliantly shines for us over 3,500 years later.

Only God has the power to take crushing defeat and to turn it over time into astounding and wondrous victory. Most people never seem to recover from these kinds of defeats. More often than not, they they endure a sentence suffering from the cumulative effects of suppression and wind up on the therapists couch with pocketfuls of prescriptions to numb their pain. God's people have been given the ability and inspiring example by Bible heroes like Joseph to understand that this life on earth is only a proving ground, not a campaign to manipulate circumstances and collect trinkets. The reality lies in the greater dimension promised to every true believer. It does not lie in the circumstances that may surround us, regardless of whether they are extraordinarily good or indescribably harsh.

Some might read the story of Joseph and think that Joseph was at his best when he commanded the armies of Egypt, or perhaps when he rescued his evil brothers and forgave them and saved his family. Others may think that Joseph was at his best when he went from slave-prisoner to Prime Minister of a mighty world empire in one day. Certainly these are the achievements of a great faith. It is my view, however, that these are not the times at which Joseph rose to his loftiest stature. Looking from God's perspective, perhaps, will cause us to see another side of Joseph—one that would appeal more to the heart of a loving Father: Joseph was at his greatest when he was in the pit, when he was in the slave-traders caravan under the desert sun headed for an unknown world and when he was in an Egyptian prison, falsely accused with no reasonable hope of ever being freed. There, in the darkness of those moments, he stepped outside the personal anguish and torment of his soul to look up to God and say in his heart, *"I LOVE YOU GOD, AND I TRUST YOU!"*

This was Joseph's greatness. So great was it, in fact, that it moved the Lord God to elevate Joseph faster, farther, higher and with greater historical consequence and impact than perhaps any other human figure whose story graces the pages of the Bible. In His great effort to get us to understand, God even tells us why:

"For the eyes of the Lord run to and fro throughout the whole earth, to show Himself strong in behalf of those whose heart is perfect toward Him."
II Chronicles 16::9

I may have taken the long way around the block in this last chapter, but it was for a reason. I wanted not just to include, but to give the fullest and most meaningful account possible of what is missing today in Fundamentalism, and beyond. Fundamentalism has become a religious quantifying and ordering of man's interpretation of God's requirements for our lives. In this strict sense, Fundamentalism shares that structure and the hierarchy it has spawned with religions such as ISLAM, and CATHOLICISM. Fundamentalism has never encouraged the building of a personal relationship with Christ that fosters a profound caring for other human beings and sustains the believer in times of trial. THIS IS THE GLORIOUS VICTORY AND EXAMPLE OF JOSEPH.

In the end, we don't need more popes. We don't need more ayatollahs. We don't need more kings in our pulpits. We have had our fill of Napoleons.

We need more Josephs. . . . !

To view the extensive Appendix to this book, please go to the book's website: PROFANEDPULPIT.COM

ABOUT THE AUTHOR

Having come to Christ as an adult in 1983, Jerry Kaifetz's life in the world was rich, diverse and exciting in many ways. He skied competitively for fifteen years in addition to three years as professional throughout Europe and the U.S.. He is a certified Master SCUBA diver with many dives in the oceans of the world. He is also an experienced yacht racer and world-class adventurer.

He owns Omega Chemical Corporation (omegachemical. com), and has developed over twenty cleaning products for industry. He also continues to write Christian books as well as secular articles on moral issues.

You can visit his ministry website at: JERRYKBOOKS. COM to read excerpts from his books and to hear his life story as produced on The Unshackled Radio Program and heard by over 3 million people in thirty-seven countries. You can also read many of his published articles on his blog at JERRYKAIFETZ.COM. He also has many videos on Youtube on a variety of social and moral issues, specializing in helping victims of abusive churches.

Profaned Pulpit has its own blog: ProfanedPulpit.org and its own YouTube channel.

OTHER BOOKS BY JERRY KAIFETZ

World Class Truth
Bible Principles in Sports & Adventure

Heroes of the Valley
The Story of Joseph
The Story of Moses
The Story of Job

Clouds Without Rain
Spiritually Ineffective Churches & How to Fix Them

The Little Drop of Water
Who Learned to Give Himself Away

Racing Toward God
My Christian Testimony

The Bench
A Heavenly Conversation

Listen to the life story of Dr. Jerry Kaifetz on the
Unshackled Radio Program

*Go to :http://jerrykbooks.com or http://unshackled.org
archived episode #A2948*

Made in the USA
Coppell, TX
16 November 2022

86487595R00108